The Student Journalist
and
FREE-LANCE WRITING

THE STUDENT JOURNALIST AND

THE
STUDENT
JOURNALIST
GUIDE
SERIES

FREE-LANCE WRITING

by

EMALENE SHERMAN

PUBLISHED BY
RICHARDS ROSEN
PRESS, INC.
NEW YORK

Library of Congress Catalog Card Number: 67-14525

Published in 1967 by Richards Rosen Press, Inc.
29 East 21st Street, New York City, N.Y. 10010

Manufactured in the United States of America

Revised Edition

Acknowledgments

I would like to thank the following persons for permission to quote information requested: Mrs. Bee Nelson, Editor, *Straight;* "Everyone Has Problems," David Raffelock, Director, The National Writers Club; Joe W. Burton, Editor, *Home Life;* Leonard R. Barnes, Associate Editor, *Motor News;* Eva H. Grant, Editor, *The PTA Magazine;* Carl Goeller, Research Director, Rust Craft Greeting Cards, Inc.; A. S. Burack, Editor, *The Writer;* members of the editorial staffs of *Seventeen, Guideposts, Ingenue,* and *Scholastic Magazines;* Chester Kerr, Director of Yale University Press; and Frederick R. Rinehart, paragraphs from *Writing Is Work* by Mary Roberts Rinehart.

About the Author

In private life, Emalene Sherman is Mrs. Justice J. Shepherd, a Cincinnati housewife. She has been a free-lance writer since she was a teenager, when her poems were published in local newspapers and in anthologies.

She earned a certificate in journalism from the University of Cincinnati Evening College and a Ph.B. degree. She was assistant supervisor of the U.C. TV-Radio Department for five years, where she wrote publicity, worked on television and radio scripts, and helped to produce programs for educational and commercial channels. She is a member of Theta Sigma Phi, national professional fraternity for women in journalism and communications.

"For three years I taught adult evening classes in writing at Colerain High School," she writes, "and I have conducted several writing workshops. I write two hours a day, five days a week, at home. Other interests are my husband and teenage son, reading, and church work."

She has sold hundreds of articles to religious, self-help, women's, travel, and baby magazines, trade journals, and miscellaneous publications: *Together, Christian Herald, The Christian Home, Hearthstone, This Day, Lookout, Home Life, Teen Talk, Straight, Success Unlimited, Life Today, Ladies' Home Companion, Woman's Life, Better Living, Motor News, Suntime, Trailways, My Baby, Baby Post, Modern Baby, American Baby, Vend, Writer's Digest,* and *Scholastic Roto.* Her articles have appeared in confession magazines: *Secrets, Real Story, Daring Romances.* The Sunday Pictorial Section of the Cincinnati Enquirer has published many of her short, humorous pieces about life in Suburbia.

To Mother, Dad, Justice, and Alan,
my constant sources of inspiration.

Contents

Chapter I

YOU CAN WRITE!

A man may write at any time if he set himself doggedly to it.

—SAMUEL JOHNSON

On a recent television program an English professor from a large university and three young writers whose work has been published were discussing "what it takes" to be an author. They did not mention education, age, status, social contacts, or geographical location.

A writer, they said, must first of all be an enthusiastic reader. Having been fascinated by the printed page since early childhood, he is always eager to learn how others think and work and play. He does not continually need to have his nose buried in a book, but he never lets a day go by without reading for at least one hour.

Secondly, a writer is *sensitive* to the moods of others. He is deeply aware of the needs of his fellow human beings and he is sympathetic toward their problems, aspirations, failures, and successes.

Third, he feels the *urge to record* what goes on around him. William Hazlitt once said that man is the only animal that laughs and weeps, for he is the only animal that is struck with the difference between what things are and what they ought to be. An author is so moved by that difference that he is impelled to pour out his feelings on paper. Simply his own feelings and opinions are worthless, however, unless he gives them universal appeal. Every piece of writing must have significance for the reader, so that he can say, "How true! That's the way it happened—or could have happened—to me." To this ingredient must be added "insight," sometimes defined as keen discernment, understanding, intuition.

Finally, the panelists said, "A lonely childhood helps. It isn't exactly essential, but it helps." Often a writer is an only child with no one close enough to him to share his thoughts. He withdraws into daydreams and eventually turns them into compositions as a substitute for companionship. Some writers come from large families, of course, but they are basically loners who seek solitude where they experience an inexplainable satisfaction from putting their nebulous thoughts into symbols the reader can understand.

Writing in some form or other is part of everyone's life. You write themes for your teachers, letters to pen pals, items for your school paper. You still wonder, though, "Can I write *creatively*? Can I earn money from my writing?" The answer to both questions is an emphatic "Yes," if you are willing to learn the rules of writing for publication and if you will doggedly apply them. Perhaps your English teacher has told you that your work is well organized and that you express yourself with originality. Assuming that you are fairly competent in constructing sentences, using correct punctuation, and developing themes from a premise to a conclusion, you have just as good a chance to earn money from your typewriter as any free-lance writer in the country. The medieval meaning of a free-lancer was a soldier who sold his services. A free-lancer was a person who acted on his own responsibility without regard to authority. Today the expression is a colloquial one that refers to a writer who is not regularly employed on any one publication.

Questions to Ask Yourself

Emerson said, "There is no luck in literary reputation." Most famous writers have certain characteristics in common. Are you destined to join their ranks? Ask yourself:

(1) *Am I an avid reader?* Read biographies of great writers and you will discover that they were readers with a purpose.

Hemingway read at least three hours each day. Read carefully several issues of the magazines for which you wish to write. Advertisements, as well as articles and stories included in them, will suggest to you the reader's age, social status, income, and general educational background. Read classics to absorb the styles of another age, and read the Bible for poetic expressions.

(2) *Am I usually aware of others' interests?* Love for your fellow man cannot be simulated; it must be genuine, real. Even if you write factual articles, you must put "heart" or understanding into your work. You make facts palatable for your reader by sugar-coating them with anecdotes, illustrations, and quotations, and the only way that you can find appropriate ones is by knowing your contemporaries. Your writing comes alive only when you are close to people and to their emotions, not reporting them second hand. Consider your family, your school, your church, your community as a stranger would see them. Look beneath the surface and you find wonder in commonplace things that others pass by every day of their lives without a second look.

(3) *Do I feel an urge to write out my observations instead of just talking about them?* Skill in writing can be acquired through persistent effort, but you must have a sense of urgency, an extra push within yourself to make you want to sit at a typewriter when ice skaters beckon on the lake or when friends in bathing suits, passing under your study window, call you to join them at a neighbor's pool. The pull to write must be so strong inside you that you are forced to write daily. You are in danger of making enemies by refusing invitations, however, for few people understand this dedication of purpose, except other writers.

Charles Dickens was once accused by a friend of avoiding her. He wrote, "Who ever is devoted to an art must be content to deliver himself wholly up to it, and to find his recompense in it. I am grieved if you suspect me of not wanting to see you, but I can't help it; I must go my way whether or no."

(4) *Do I like to work alone?* Writing is a solitary business.

You must shut yourself away from people, the telephone, the radio, and TV. While you may have trained yourself to study with the radio or record player blaring in your ear, you cannot write logically unless distractions are kept to a minimum. In the final analysis, you face a blank sheet of paper and if it is ever to be filled with words, you must work without interruptions. In modern ranch-style homes there is very little privacy. A family room is used by all members of the household for recreation, and bedrooms often are shared with brothers or sisters. You can find a nook for you alone, though, if you look for it and if you enlist your parents' co-operation. This could be a desk in a corner of your bedroom, a secluded section of the basement, or part of the attic, that fast-disappearing upstairs retreat especially conducive to writing on rainy days.

To the panelists' observations, I would add two other points:

(5) *Do I enjoy gathering material?* You not only learn from other people, but you get information from reference books and encyclopedias. A writer's favorite haunt is his local library. A straight "A" in English composition does not guarantee your success as a writer. Many college professors have never written a book, and several great writers did not go beyond grade school. This does not mean that you should not get as much formal education as possible, but you should also know how to supplement your knowledge quickly and how to use it in the most effective way. Try to be, as James Joyce said, a person on whom "nothing is wasted." Learn from every experience; that is another way of gathering material for writing. From the age of fourteen, Sherwood Anderson earned his living in Ohio cabbage fields, racing stables, and factories. He was a successful manager of an Ohio paint factory when he left it in his middle thirties to write about persons and situations he knew well. Herman Melville had to leave school at fifteen because his father went bankrupt. He became a bank clerk, a farmer, and a teacher; and at seventeen he shipped as a cabin boy to Liverpool. This voyage, and subsequent ones, supplied ideas for *Moby Dick* and other works.

(6) *Do I have an orderly mind?* Most persons let conversations, reading matter, sounds, smells, tastes, and feelings leak through their sievelike minds and dissolve into nothingness. A writer must grasp every grain and put it where he can find it again. He needs either a physical filing system or a mental one that he can go to when he needs examples to illustrate points in a manuscript. William Faulkner said in an interview that everything a person has ever "touched, read, tasted, smelled, heard, or done since infancy influences him in some degree, and that is all reflected in the work which that man does."

Opportunities for Writers

If your answers are "Yes" to the above questions, you have the basic qualifications for entering a field where opportunities are unlimited.

More than $20 billion is spent each year on the communications industry, based almost entirely on the written word. Writers are needed in advertising, television, radio, public relations, newspaper work, and movies. As a teenager still living at home with your parents, you have your food, clothing, and shelter furnished. *Now* is the time for you to learn the writing business by working at home. Most professional writers hold down a full-time job in addition to their free-lance writing, because the income of authors is uncertain. Experts say that you should not try to be a full-time writer until you have enough money saved to support you for one year. You "have it made" if you get an allowance, because it will cover your expenses until you start collecting checks.

Hundreds of magazines are published in this country each month. Some of them are devoted exclusively to such topics as religion, science, art, hobbies, travel, bicycles, interplanetary flight—almost any subject you care to mention. Weekly newspapers number 9,000 and dailies 2,000. Many of them carry magazine sections. The 1,100 active publishing houses in the United States publish more than 13,000 new non-fiction titles and editions a year. More than 500 local stations and television networks use scripts at an alarming rate. Who writes verses for the 5¼ billion greeting cards that go through the mails each year? Someone, somewhere, every day is cashing checks from editors, and it might as well be you!

Your first task is to decide *what kind of writing you wish to do*. Some of us are versatile enough to write essays, poetry, articles, short stories, and novels, but the average person finds that he must specialize. He does not have time to try all types of writing; more important, he is capable of doing one particular type better than any other. What do you like to read? Poetry? Short stories? Essays? You will probably want to write the kind of material you enjoy reading. Each has its own technique. Nonfiction is easiest for the beginner to master, and today more articles are published than short stories.

Next, think about the audience you wish to reach. How large is your vocabulary? What is the message you hope to share with your reader? You would not use the same words or the same topics when writing for children that you would for college graduates.

Consider the type of magazine that might publish your material. If you are aiming at the slicks, you need a sophisticated command of language. If you are trying to sell to the pulps, you can use simpler words. (But do not make the mistake of thinking that sloppy, ungrammatical writing will be acceptable here. You still must write well.) If you are aiming at the quality publications, your tone will be entirely different. The best way to find out what each magazine buys is to read several issues of that publication.

What are your chances of saying something original, now that millions of words in the form of magazines, books, newspapers, pamphlets, and scripts pour forth from our presses every day? It has been estimated that it would take all the people in the world over a thousand million years to write all the possible combinations of the 26 letters of the alphabet. Mathematics is not my strong point, but I believe that comes to something like

620, followed by 27 zeros. That is why it will always be possible for someone to say something original as long as language endures.

What You Are, Not Who You Are

Writers come in assorted shapes and sizes, of various ages and abilities. You can write on a desert island, or in a Manhattan apartment. Edna St. Vincent Millay was fourteen when her first poem was published in a national magazine. She gained recognition at twenty for "Renascence." Edgar Allan Poe and Françoise Sagan made their names in their teens, as did Pamela Moore with her novel, *Chocolates for Breakfast*. Stephen Crane, Truman Capote, and William Saroyan became famous while they were still in their early twenties. When John Keats was orphaned at fifteen he was apprenticed to a surgeon, but he devoted himself to books and to writing. Enjoying little honor in his short life (he died at twenty-six), he saw his books condemned and savagely attacked in literary reviews of his day. Robert Southey wrote an epic poem, *Joan of Arc,* when he was nineteen. Stephen Foster composed a song when he was thirteen. Yet, Goethe was past eighty when he completed *Faust*. Thomas Hardy and George Bernard Shaw were still writing when they were approaching ninety. W. Somerset Maugham wrote best sellers in his late seventies and Agatha Christie, a grandmother many times, continued to turn out detective novels.

Apparently a love for writing lasts a lifetime. Maybe you will never become a famous novelist or a superlative short-story writer. You may never see the inside of a newspaper office or a magazine editor's inner sanctum; your book might never appear on a best-seller list, yet there is no more rewarding occupation, even if it remains only a hobby, than making words do your bidding on paper.

If you are a boy, you might enter another profession and still keep writing as a sideline. Ministers often write for religious publications; doctors contribute to medical journals; lawyers write articles related to their field; sociologists and psychologists tell all in print about how to live a happier, fuller life. Zane Grey was a dentist. A. J. Cronin was a physician. Erle Stanley Gardner was first a lawyer, then a writer. Robert Travers was a judge when he wrote *Anatomy of a Murder*. Jonathan Swift was dean of a church when he penned *Gulliver's Travels*. Lewis Carroll of *Alice in Wonderland* fame was a mathematician.

If you are a girl, you might soon be a housewife and mother. Writing is a good hobby to pursue in your spare time. Margaret Mitchell was a housewife when she wrote *Gone With the Wind*. Grace Metalious wrote *Peyton Place* in-between household chores. Jean Kerr, who launched a whole new career for herself by writing *Please Don't Eat the Daisies,* once said that she escaped her five children's demands by locking herself in her car to write.

How to Get Started

You can start today to become a writer by keeping a diary. Most teenagers have one under lock and key; it is their own special listening post that guards secrets they cannot bear to tell aloud and they have no intention of seeing it published. Some famous ones have appeared in print, however, and they make entertaining reading for other authors; read *Confessions of Saint Augustine, Confessions of Rousseau,* the *Diary of Samuel Pepys,* and the *Diary of Anne Frank*. Autobiography is the simplest form of literature. The cardinal rule of writing is *write about what you know,* and whom do you know better than yourself?

Two advantages to keeping a diary are:

(1) *You are forced to write every day*. Through writing you rise above disappointments, sickness, financial reverses; working with words leads you ever upward and onward to a better understanding of yourself and of others. The very act of keeping a diary encourages you to develop your gift of observation. Try to record one line of beauty expressed in your own unique way, instead of ordinary statements, such as, "Saw Tom today. He's

dreamy." Here is a poetic excerpt from Katharine Mansfield's *Journal*:

> The moon is rising but the reluctant day lingers upon the sea and sky. The sea is dabbled with a pink the colour of unripe cherries, and in the sky there is a flying yellow light like the wings of canaries. Very stubborn and solid are the trunks of the palm trees. Springing from their tops the stiff green bouquets seem to cut into the evening air and among them, the blue gum trees, tall and slender with sickle-shaped leaves and drooping branches half blue, half violet. The moon is just over the mountain behind the village. The dogs know she is there; already they begin to howl and bark. The fishermen are shouting and whistling to one another as they bring in their boats, some young boys are singing in half-broken voices down by the shore, and there is a noise of children crying, little children with burnt cheeks and sand between their toes being carried to bed . . .

But not all of her days were happy. Every writer has times when he feels useless to humanity and inadequate to meet life's demands. Miss Mansfield was continually depressed by illness, isolation, and the sound of the sea. One day she confessed, "And even in my brain, in my head, I can think and act and write wonders—wonders; but the moment I really try to put them down I fail miserably." *

What is annoying you today? Write it out, and you will feel better within the hour, for writing is a therapy akin to airing your problems on a psychiatrist's couch.

(2) *Incidents you record can be expanded later.* On days when you are pushed for time, you might write only a line or two, but those few words can stimulate your thinking at a later date. Arnold Bennett once observed two old ladies having tea and he wrote down their description while it was fresh in his mind. Later he used them as characters in *The Old Wives' Tale.*

* *Journal of Katharine Mansfield* edited by J. Middleton Murry, Alfred A. Knopf, N.Y., 1941, p. 66.

He was a methodical man, as shown in this entry in his diary: "This year I have written 335,340 words, grand total: 224 articles and stories."

Your Tools

Like any other trade, writing requires specific tools. You should have:

A typewriter. If you do not own one, you could borrow or rent one until you start earning money. If you have never learned how to type, take a typing course at your school or teach yourself touch typing in your spare time. It is best, however, for you to join a class, because there you get the benefit of drills that build up speed.

A knowledge of shorthand or speedwriting. For a person who goes into newspaper work, this is an essential qualification. A free-lancer can work without this skill, but it is especially valuable to save time during interviews and when you are getting information at the library. Some writers compose in longhand. A manuscript should be typed, however, before it is submitted to an editor. He is too busy to try to decipher hand-written manuscripts.

Reference books. Keep your dictionary near you when you write. No one is infallible in the use of words and even professionals refer to their dictionary. You might also find Roget's *Thesaurus* useful, as well as a book of quotations. (*Bartlett's Quotations* comes in a paperback edition.) Make it a habit to watch for other paperbacks in drug stores, supermarkets, and in book stores that will aid you in getting background information on such subjects as stones and minerals, trees, stars, campcraft, etc. Knowing where to go for reference material when you need it in a hurry is more important than trying to cram your head full of facts that you would soon forget anyway. If you have a set of encyclopedias, use them; if not, go to the library. Sometimes a librarian will supply information you request on the telephone.

Stationery. You need a supply of bond paper, second sheets, carbon paper, 9x12 manila envelopes, and #10 envelopes. If a manuscript is five pages or less, you can fold it and send it in #10 envelopes. If it runs over five pages, mail it flat.

Stamps. Always enclose a self-addressed envelope with enough postage for the return of your manuscript, in case the editor cannot use it. Check at your post office about the Special Fourth Class Rate for manuscripts.

A file. Keep a carbon copy of every manuscript you submit to an editor, with a notation as to where you sent it, the date, how much you received for it, or, if it was rejected, make a note why the editor did not buy it. Someday you will have enough money to buy a file cabinet, but for the time being you can use a desk drawer, an oversize manila envelope, or a big box hidden under your bed for filing your carbons.

You will also find it helpful to have a pack of 3x5 cards, a stapler, pencils, a typing eraser, and a box of paper clips.

Rules for Writing

To achieve publication of any kind of writing, you should observe the following rules:

(1) *Carry a small notebook with you wherever you go.* When you ride the school bus, you often overhear conversations that could be used in articles and stories. Jot them down. You hear jokes, epigrams, pet peeves. Record them on the spot. You think you will remember them, but too many facts will crowd into your mind before the day is over. Short stories appear before your eyes every day at the soda fountain, in the lunchroom, in hallways at school, on streets, and in homes. You cannot afford to let them elude your grasp.

(2) *Keep a file of ideas.* Each day clip at least one article from the newspaper that suggests something to write about. Collect cartoons, clip magazines, save letters—anything that starts your imagination working. A file folder is the most convenient way of saving ideas.

(3) *Write on schedule.* Most prolific writers stick to the same working hours week in and week out. Thomas Mann wrote from

breakfast until noon, slowly, in longhand, seven days a week. His average production was about a page and a quarter of manuscript each day. Just think, if you wrote only 250 words a day, five days a week, you would have 65,250 words at the end of 261 working days. That is enough writing for a full-length novel!

Since you are in the busiest years of your life, you cannot write as often as you might wish. Your school work comes first. That consumes most of your day until three o'clock. If you go to bed at ten, let's say, you have seven hours left. The time allotted for homework varies, according to assignments and how many study hall periods you have. During examination time, of course, you spend every free moment cramming. As a rule, however, you spend an average of two hours per day on homework. Count another two hours for dinner and personal grooming and an hour for outside activity or watching TV; that leaves you two hours for writing. Obviously, school activities, such as football games, basketball games, team practice, and school dances, will interrupt your writing, as will church meetings, sickness, or home parties. Even if you are not athletic and do not participate in many activities outside school, you have little free time. Your main problem, as a writer, is to make use of the time you do have to the best of your ability. Perhaps, now, the only time you have to write is on Saturday mornings or Friday evenings or Sunday afternoon. Set aside that time to put your writing into some form. Whether your interest lies in poetry, articles, short stories, fillers, plays, television scripts, or books, the general approach is the same. You must map out your own schedule. It is essential to have one.

An inspirational motto, where you can see it every day, helps to spur you on when you are overtaken by a writer's slump. Mine is a quotation from Calvin Coolidge pasted in the front of my notebook:

> Nothing in the world can take the place of persistence. Talent will not; nothing is more common than unsuccessful men with talent. Genius will not; unrewarded genius is almost a proverb. Education will not; the world is full of educated derelicts. Persistence and

determination alone are omnipotent. The slogan "Press On" has solved and always will solve the problems of the human race.

(4) *Read with an eye toward having your own work published.* It is one thing to read for pleasure, but it is quite another to read with an analytical mind that asks: "Why did the publisher buy this piece of writing? Why did it appear in this particular magazine? Why did I feel emotional satisfaction when I finished reading it? Could I write something similar to it?" Try to pattern your material along the lines of what is published, but use a slightly different approach. Do not imitate. Look for magazines using subjects you are interested in: hot-rods, model cars, the problems of dating, opportunities for careers, new dance steps, music, changing styles. Maybe you subscribe to one or more of them. If not, buy them at the newsstands, or check their contents in your library.

(5) *Do not talk about your writing.* This is one of the most dangerous pitfalls that writers can tumble into; they kill their ideas by discussing them with a friend. You expend your enthusiasm in talking and you have none left for writing. With the best intentions in the world, a friend might try to "help" you by offering suggestions that ruin your artistic design. He could even persuade you to drop a project entirely, when in reality it is an excellent one that should be written out and published. You must write the way you prefer to do it, because you can best communicate your enthusiasm only if you are on fire with the idea.

(6) *Mail your manuscripts to editors; do not hide them in a drawer.* Be sure that they are neatly typed and are accompanied by a self-addressed envelope and postage. (See chapter on Marketing.)

(7) *Believe in yourself.* If you do not have faith in yourself, no one else will. I have taken all the courses in literature, English composition, and creative writing offered at my alma mater. The inspiration and encouragement that my professors gave me would have amounted to nothing if I had not believed deep within myself that I could write.

You are obligated to throw your whole personality into what you write. Only in mastering the discipline necessary to control your mind can you effectively share your thoughts with others. Writing requires discipline, self-control, orderliness, enthusiasm.

You can write if *you* believe that you can!

Chapter II

WHERE TO FIND IDEAS

Ye who write, choose a subject suited to your abilities.

—HORACE

I once spent six months living in an isolated cabin on a New Jersey lake. There was no telephone, no mail delivery, not even a milkman's footsteps to break the silence. Homes surrounding me had been boarded up for the winter. No voices, no cars, no television. The only tracks in the snow were made by an occasional rabbit. A perfect retreat for a writer? I had a typewriter, but I did not write a line. Silence drummed against my ears; boredom and solitude crushed my spirit.

Do not think that you must live in an isolated sanctuary to be a writer. Solitude is necessary when you are working at the typewriter, but it is equally important to circulate among people to find out what they are talking about, what they are reading, what their dreams are. To preserve in permanent form the loves, hates, anticipations, disappointments, joys and sorrows of your generation, you need contact with that generation to increase your awareness of their problems.

Writing does not always flow easily. At times it is difficult even to fill one page. That is why you must constantly replenish your wellspring of creativity by alternately mingling with the crowd and then withdrawing from it to read and to contemplate.

WHERE DO IDEAS COME FROM?

(1) *Relatives.* You are in conflict with your parents a great deal of the time, since you are struggling to grow up. You want

to make your own decisions and to leave your childhood behind, while your parents try to protect you by giving advice based on their own experiences. Feeling that you are misunderstood by the older generation might be your best asset toward becoming a writer. Emerson once said, "Pythagoras was misunderstood, and Socrates, and Jesus, and Luther, and Copernicus, and Galileo, and Newton, and every pure and wise spirit that ever took flesh. To be great is to be misunderstood." If you are angry enough to have deep feelings about yourself and the persons who cross your path, if you are angry enough to express your thoughts in words and to offer satisfactory solutions to universal problems, if you are angry enough to want to change conditions, you can be an effective writer because what you write matters deeply to you. A writer must *care* about what he writes.

Conflict is necessary in a short story; it can also be the basis for an article. Although you frequently disagree with parents, grandparents, aunts, uncles, cousins, brothers, and sisters, you cannot always express your thoughts aloud; for, after all, you have to live with some of them part of the time. Writing your opinions and collecting checks for them is much more rewarding than open warfare. One girl who thought her grandmother was mistaken when she said that if a mother visited a zoo before her child was born, he would be marked for life, wrote an article called "Don't You Believe It," exploding that and several other myths about childbirth. She sold it to a baby magazine.

Keep your mouth closed and your ears open when you are in the company of older adults. Little will they suspect that they are supplying you with money-making ideas!

(2) *Friends.* Whether you are a gregarious person with many friends, or a quiet person who carefully chooses only one or two close associates, you need a viewpoint other than your own. Jot down others' ideas in that little notebook you carry when they talk about sports, hobbies, clothes, cars, parental restrictions. You might not get around to working on those ideas until some Saturday morning, but just seeing them in black and white will

start you to thinking when you do have time to sit down at the typewriter.

Sometimes you are affected by what happens to your friends. Suppose you see a boy being paddled at school and you think that the punishment is unjustified. Talk to him, to his parents, to the teacher, and to other students. You could write an article, "Whipping Is Outmoded." On the other hand, if the boy is a bully and other disciplinary methods have failed to bring him into line, so that he has become a menace to other students in the classroom, you might do an article, "Sometimes Paddling Is Necessary."

When you attempt to capture your friends' personalities, peculiarities, and problems on paper, you are giving your work what every writer strives for: Universal Appeal. The persons you know have some of the same desires, frustrations, hopes, dreams, ambitions, disappointments of other human beings. They are a never-ending source of article ideas.

(3) *Personal experience*. Religious magazines, self-help digests, women's magazines, men's magazines, the confessions and Sunday supplements all use personal experience stories. Study the "First Person Articles" in *The Reader's Digest*. An article for this series must be a true, hitherto unpublished narrative of an unusual personal experience, either dramatic, inspirational or humorous. It would bring you $2,500, but there are smaller markets to try if you fail with this one. You have much less competition in lesser magazines that do not receive so many unsolicited manuscripts.

Do you have a summer job? Other teenagers would be interested in knowing how you went about getting it. You could write an article entitled, "How I Found a Summer Job." Maybe you would like to express your views on driving ("Teenage Drivers *Are* Careful") or on music ("Musicians Are Not Sissies"). Regardless of what part of the country you live in, what your home life is like, or where you go to school, you have at least one experience each day to write about. Louisa May Alcott worked both at home and in domestic service. From the age of sixteen she wrote with no success, until she received $200 for her hospital sketches about her work as a volunteer nurse in Georgetown. None of her scribbling during her early years was in vain, for when she was thirty-six years old, *Little Women,* based on the experiences of her own family, brought her fame and fortune.

(4) *Newspaper items.* Every day when your family is finished reading the newspaper, clip at least one idea from it that you think could be developed into an article. Make up several file folders according to subject matter, and after you have had time to gather more information, you can expand the ideas into salable pieces. Good sources of ideas are medical columns, the religious writings of Dr. Norman Vincent Peale, Dr. Billy Graham, and Bishop Fulton Sheen, as well as editorials. So are advice-to-the-lovelorn columns, such as, "Dear Abby," and letters to the editor. Recently, a father wrote a letter to a newspaper deploring drinking at teenage parties. He cited a specific party his daughter had attended where beer and hard liquor flowed freely. In answer to his question about what is happening to the morals of teenagers, another reader wrote in to the column and said that the blame rests squarely on parents, who have liquor in the home and make it available to their children. If a writer cared to follow up this subject, he could interview the men who wrote the letters, parents, friends, and perhaps his clergyman. Some of the articles I have written that were prompted by a newspaper item are:

"You Can Earn Money At Home"
"Space Age Prayer"
"How to Guard Against Headaches"
"Don't Skim Through Life"
"How to Cope With Shade"

(5) *Observation.* A writer never tires of watching people at football games, in bus terminals, in stores, on the street. He is curious about what makes them live and move and have their

activities. When I was lying in a hospital bed with a leg in traction, I watched a workman cleaning a fan in my room. He took great pride in doing a thorough job and I wondered why he was so particular about doing his menial task well. We struck up a conversation. He told me that when he was in the Navy he learned that if he did not do something right the first time, he had to do it over. Through his actions I re-learned a long-forgotten lesson: anything worth doing at all is worth doing well. On that slender thread I built an article called "The Man Who Cleaned the Fan."

Every article you write grows out of four steps: (a) Observing (b) Recording (c) Weighing the facts (d) Choosing a viewpoint.

(6) *Classified telephone directory*. Are there any unusual businesses in your town? Read the yellow pages of the telephone book to get ideas for articles that you might sell to specialized publications. I once visited a mink ranch and wrote an article on the care and feeding of the animals and what happens to them from the time they leave their cages until they become pelts. Make an appointment to talk to local businessmen; they will be glad to work with you on writing about their specialty. Florists, jewelers, grocers, and other tradespeople read trade journals in their field that need material on new methods of merchandising. They welcome any publicity you can bring to their store.

(7) *Interviews.* If a celebrity comes to your town, arrange to interview him. But do not overlook interviews with persons you know who are not famous. You could talk to an ornithologist and sell your article to a nature magazine. Do you know someone who collects coins or stamps? Do you know a ham radio operator? Are you acquainted with a woman who makes unusual quilts or doll clothes? Hobby articles sell to several types of magazines, besides to those dedicated exclusively to hobbies.

When you are interviewing someone, keep these points in mind:

(a) Plan your questions ahead of time, so that you can draw forth specific answers to them.

(b) Learn all you can about your interviewee before you meet him. What is his background? What has he achieved? You can obtain information from published biographical material if he is famous, or from talks with friends, relatives, and business associates.
(c) Identify yourself when you call for a definite appointment. Give your name, the school you attend, and tell why you want the interview.
(d) Be on time.
(e) Keep your notebook inconspicuous. Some persons "clam up" if they think you are taking down every word they say. Make your notes brief and fill them in as soon as you arrive home.
(f) Check the spelling of all names, titles, and addresses.
(g) Keep your questions short and simple.
(h) If your article needs pictures, ask your interviewee for them, with a promise that they will be returned.
(i) Take his phone number and tell him you will let him know when the article appears. Explain that since you are a free-lance writer, you do not know as yet what publication will use it, but that you will see that he gets a copy when it is published.
(j) Be sure to thank him for his time.

(8) *Books and magazines.* Many professional writers get their best ideas when they are reading what someone else has written. This is not to say that they copy ideas; often they take the exact opposite viewpoint from that of the author. You naturally disagree with some of the things you see in print. One writer who read an article about how irresponsible young people are today was so moved that he wrote one emphasizing how he thought young people are superior to the youths of his father's day. It sold to a national magazine.

State your beliefs with conviction, backed up with statistics, quotes based on interviews with authorities, and anecdotes. You might turn the nation's trend of thought in a new direction.

(9) *The World Almanac.* Every year a new edition of this book of facts appears on your newsstand. It contains information

on every subject from "Agriculture" on down to Z. Even though you have no special topic in mind to write about, just thumbing through this book will stimulate your imagination. A girl who noticed in the almanac that the following year would be leap year, wrote, "It's Leap Year, Girls!" and sold it the first time she sent it to an editor because her timing was just right.

(10) *Government Pamphlets.* To receive a free bi-weekly listing of "Selected United States Government Publications," send your name and address on a postcard, with your request to be put on their mailing list, to:

U.S. Government Printing Office
Division of Public Documents
Washington, D.C. 20402

The pamphlets cover a variety of topics, such as community craft programs, housing, the United Nations, homemaking, child care. Besides giving you new ideas for articles, the pamphlets are a short cut to gathering background material. You can order them on a special form provided for any price from 5 cents on up, with the average being about 25 cents.

(11) *Conversations.* The writer listens much more than he talks. Listen to others and you learn what they think is important and how they feel on topics of current interest. You discover what annoys them, what pleases them, what they want to do about their personal life, and how they hope to improve the state of the world. Some of my published articles that grew out of conversations are:

"How to Treat Your Stepchild"
"Don't Stay Home on Your Vacation"
"Spoiled—or Just Loved?"
"Why Does Infidelity Flourish?"

Not only women are the talkative ones in our society; boys and men pour forth their views in a never-subsiding torrent on streetcorners, in cars, over a coke at the drug counter, in gas stations, at church meetings, in bull sessions at school or at home.

How Good Is Your Idea?

After you have decided what to write about, ask yourself if that idea will be interesting to readers six months from now. *Most magazines work at least six months ahead.* You can sell a Christmas article in June and a summer travel article in December. Many manuscripts are rejected, not because they are poorly written, but because they arrived too late to be included in the editor's schedule.

Would you read an article on the subject you have in mind? If you were looking through a magazine, would you pause long enough to give it a second glance? What type of periodical would be most likely to use your article? Get a copy of that magazine and read it with an eye toward topics covered, word-length, style of writing, and slant of the publication (toward parents, children, senior citizens?).

Next, check the *Reader's Guide to Periodical Literature* in the library to see what has been published on the subject in recent months. Even if your idea has been worked over many times by other writers, you can sell it if your angle is sufficiently fresh and new.

A question that always occurs to writers is, "Should I query an editor about my idea, or should I send him the completed manuscript?" Personally, I have never sold an article on a query. I go ahead and complete the article, especially if it is a short one. Then I submit it to an editor, for I feel that a letter and an outline do not do my idea justice. This is a matter of personal preference. If your manuscripts run over 1,500 words, you may prefer to get the green light from an editor before putting hours of work into them.

What to Avoid

Topics to stay away from are not taboos, in the sense that an article praising dancing or alcoholic beverages would not sell to a religious magazine; they are topics *unwanted* by editors simply because they know their readers better than you do. The average person reads for entertainment, for information from someone who knows more about a subject than he does, for instruction on how-to-do-it projects, or for just plain escape. He is not interested in *articles that fail to present anything new*.

If your idea is not new, you are better off to leave it alone. Nothing is *new* in the strictest sense of the word, but your approach to it must be unique, different, full of information not previously exploited. An article a writer did on divorce came back from an editor with a note that she had had too many manuscripts on the subject. The writer's angle was not sufficiently different to warrant publishing it. In thinking over the magazines he had read in recent months, he realized that none of the divorce material had been aimed at the person perhaps most seriously affected by a split in the family: the child. He rewrote his material with a teenager in mind. "If Your Parents Are Divorced . . ." tackled from this viewpoint problems arising from a broken home and offered the teenager some solutions for solving them. It sold the first time out to a teen magazine.

Articles that are too factual. When beginning writers learn that articles should be loaded with statistics and that they should have reams of information about their subjects that do not even appear in the finished product, they tend to cram too many facts into their final draft. You cannot over-research a topic, of course, but it is possible to knock the reader over the head with so many figures that he does not care to finish reading the article. The best way to break up factual information is to intersperse it with anecdotes, illustrations, and quotations to add human interest.

Articles that describe your darling pets . . . or relatives . . . or home. Sometimes such an article comes off all right if it is written in a humorous vein, but very few of us are capable of writing really good humor. Editors avoid "think pieces" that offer no help to the reader. A few pet magazines use articles on cats, dogs, birds, and fish. Some publications have room for the "unforgettable character" sketch. As a rule, however, editors strive to give readers what they want: help in solving problems within their own families. Unless you are a well-known, established writer, do not write an article just to enjoy yourself; you will be the only one who is entertained.

Articles that insult the reader. Never suggest that your reader is anything but charming, interesting, alert, well-educated and attractive. Do not talk down to him. Articles giving advice are especially difficult to write without sounding preachy. Avoid saying, "Believe me," or "I know what I'm talking about." Uplift him. Inspire him. Write in such a way that he thinks *he* is the one who uncovered these gems of wisdom, not you.

Articles with a negative viewpoint. Today's audience wants you to accentuate the positive. Their daily newspaper and television shows bring them enough topics to worry about. Of course, you cannot hide your true self when you write, and if you are a pessimist, your pessimism shows. Suppose you attend a party that is a flop and you decide to write an article on "How Not to Give a Party." Maybe you could carry it off all right, but your chances of making a sale would be increased if you took the positive approach, "How to Give a Successful Party."

You learn what sells only through the trial-and-error method. Remember, *no writing you do is ever wasted!* With every line you write, you grow in facility of expression.

Put It on Paper

A friend of mine has called me several times to outline articles that she hopes to write. Her voice over the telephone is full of enthusiasm. She fairly bubbles with excitement. The conversations last almost an hour. Invariably her ideas sound like salable material, but she has never sold an article and I doubt if she ever will. Why? Because although she unmistakably has something to say, she does not *say it in print.* I am her only audience, and I do not pay her for her time.

When you have an idea, write it down. Then type your notes. Next, jot down a brief outline so that you will have a clear picture of how you are going to handle your material. Do not spend too much time on a detailed outline, however, or you will lose your sparkle. It is sufficient to make a list of the main points you want to cover. Type a rough draft while the idea is "hot." Then put your manuscript away for a few days for a cooling-off period. Again I say, *don't talk about what you intend to write*. It is your secret, shared with no one, until it is published.

The only exception is the reading of your manuscript to a writers' class. If there is one in your community, you can get help from other writers on how to improve your writing and where to market your work. But stay away from those time-killers, writers' clubs, where members get together to talk about writing as a substitute for getting down to work.

Universal Appeal

Here is where rules end, for everyone has his own particular way of developing his ideas. You will have to rework your article several times before it is polished enough to mail to an editor. Maybe you are one of the lucky ones who can type it twice and have a completed manuscript. My magic number is three. I never achieve a finished article without at least three typings.

The articles that appeal most to readers are those that have what editors call hit-homeness. What interests a human being most? Himself. In a group picture, whose face do you look for first? Your own. What articles do you read in a magazine? The ones that have special significance for you. For example, the following appeared in the April, 1963 issue of *Ingenue,* because that magazine is slanted toward teenagers: "No's and Yes's for Teens," "Is Censorship Fair to Teens?" and "Beauty Notes from Top Teen Models."

If you can show your reader that you have suffered through the same experiences he has and that you have found happiness in spite of problems, he will literally eat your words.

One of my professors at the University of Cincinnati, Dr. Victor E. Reichert, once said to our journalism class, "Behind every piece of writing there must be a *real* person." That statement is deceptively simple. Naturally you are a "real" person of conviction who believes in what he has to say. But he meant also that a writer must be an understanding, unselfish person working with love, devotion and sincerity to touch the minds of other men.

When you take your manuscript out of the drawer for rewriting, check it for universal appeal. If it is too narrow in its outlook, change it now before an editor sees it. Be sure that every paragraph is necessary. No point is too small to study for accuracy, no word is too precious not to be cut, no statement is too valuable not to be struck out if it does not contribute something worth-while to the whole composition.

No one has ever improved upon Aristotle's plot formula stated in three simple words in his *Poetics*: a beginning, a middle, and an end. You can find those words elaborated upon in almost every book on writing. Aristotle said that a *beginning* requires something to follow it; an *end* supposes something to precede it; a *middle* supposes something to precede and requires something to follow. An article, too, must have these ingredients.

He also said that whatever is beautiful must not only have its parts arranged in a certain manner, "but must also be of a certain Magnitude; for beauty consists in Magnitude and Order."

A writer is an orderly person who sifts the important from the unimportant, universal truths from insignificant ideas. He is detached enough from his surroundings to realize that he is most proficient at recording what goes on in his own back yard.

The more you search for things to write about, the more ideas will come to you without your ever leaving home. Emily Dickinson wrote more than 1,500 poems on old envelopes and paper bags, and she hid them in bureau drawers. She asked her sister to burn them after her death, but luckily they were preserved and subsequently published. Like Miss Dickinson, you can find your best ideas all around you. The difference between you and her is that *you* are going to try to see your work published during your lifetime.

Chapter III

START WITH ARTICLES

That writer does the most, who gives his reader the most *knowledge and takes from him the* least *time.*

—C. C. COLTON

In an informal essay, "Every Man's Natural Desire to Be Somebody Else," Samuel McChord Crothers tells about a young man coming to his study with a manuscript he wanted criticized. He said it was a short piece that would not take much of Crothers' time. "In fact it is only the first chapter," he said, "in which I explain the Universe." *

All of us have sudden flashes when we feel we could explain the meaning of life in a way that has never been attempted before. These flashes of inspiration, said Crothers, usually occur about four o'clock in the morning, and "Having explained the Universe, we relapse into satisfied slumber. When a few hours later, we rise, we wonder what the explanation was."

A serious writer keeps a notebook beside his bed to write down thoughts when they come to him. The professional captures ideas in flight and writes with the purpose of selling them. The amateur allows fleeting thoughts to get away; in rare moments he is content to scribble in secret with no disciplined rewriting designed to reach an audience. Resolve now that you will take the professional approach to your writing.

* *The College Reader,* edited by Robert Morss Lovett and Howard Mumford Jones, Houghton Mifflin Co., Boston, 1936, p. 185.

File Cards

Even an author as accomplished as Dickens had to have a system for filing words and phrases, for he once said, "When found, make a note of." Succinct advice!

Only you can discover the system best suited to your working habits. Some writers favor what a friend of mine calls the "jacket" system. They use large envelopes for filing every scrap of information relating to one article, from a news clipping to a carbon of the finished manuscript. Others use file folders. I use folders only for miscellaneous clippings that are too large to reduce to a 3x5 card and for copies of different types of publications. For example, if I am writing a religious article, I can look in the folder labeled "Religious Magazines" for a typical publication in that field. Looking through the kind of magazine you are writing for refreshes your memory about the slant the editors prefer.

File cards are the quickest and easiest means of keeping information at your finger-tips. I have a box of 3x5 cards on which I type quotes from famous authors, statistics taken from books, newspapers, and pamphlets; names, dates—in short, any notes that might be useful in the future. I always give the source. A typical card looks like this:

> From the *Journal of Katharine Mansfield,* p. 119: "I have discovered that I cannot burn the candle at one end and write a book with the other."

Here is a quote I took down in shorthand from a TV show:

> You can't paint when the mood strikes; you must paint every day if you want to be a painter. If you want to be an actor, you must act every day. You can't be a week-end flyer and be a good flyer. I recently heard a very fine writer say that he puts a piece of paper in the typewriter whether he feels like writing or not.
>
> —Jack Lord
> May 18, 1962
> *Here's Hollywood*

If I see a quotation on a calendar, in a magazine, or in the newspaper and do not want to take time to type it, I clip it and tape it to a card. Here is one:

> Nothing is particularly
> hard if you divide
> it into small jobs.
> —Schiller

Make your own divisions. They are easy to discard or to replace as you expand your horizons. At the moment mine are:

Authors
Books re: Writing
Miscellaneous Facts
Pending (Articles that are out to editors)*
Quotes—Famous Persons
Sold*

Students in my writing classes are often discouraged when I tell them the deliberate, systematic, down-to-earth attitude I take toward writing. "Such a lot of work!" they say. Secretly they are disappointed to learn that writing *is* work, because they thought that a writer simply sat at his desk and let his thoughts flow onto the paper before him. Certainly uninspired writing will not sell, but neither will inspiration alone produce an article worthy of publication.

An article is not an essay. It has a structure all its own.

Essays vs. Articles

The modern feature article is an off-shoot of the essay. You remember reading Montaigne's essays or those of Lamb and Bacon. No doubt you have written essays in school. They are short compositions that are chiefly the result of one individual's living, reading and thinking. The word essay means an "attempt"

* See chapter on Marketing.

(*essai*) and it originally implied that the writer set out to open up a subject informally; he was not obliged to discuss it with completeness. Montaigne retired from active life while he was still under forty to live in quiet and to devote the remainder of his life to reading and writing. In 1580 he published his first edition of essays. He wrote, "Myself am the groundwork of my book."

Although you put yourself into your articles, no one would buy them if you wrote about yourself alone. Today there is a very limited market for essays. You see them occasionally in *Harpers, The Atlantic,* or *American Mercury*. An essay explores a single subject at leisure. Its tone is quiet and gentle. It stimulates the reader's thinking with a well-polished style and a superior vocabulary.

Ever since World War II, readers have increasingly turned toward magazine articles that give them the facts in an interesting, compact style. We are a nation in a hurry and we want to get information in the quickest possible way. The main differences between essays and articles are that in an article . . .

(1) You can state your theme in one sentence.
(2) You use word pictures, anecdotes, facts, statistics, and figures to expand that theme.
(3) You give your reader a statement to remember, a final summing up, an ending that goes out where you came in.

To accomplish that end, you must start with an outline.

"I hadn't thought about wasting my talents on facts," you say? Contrary to popular opinion, article writing *is* creative. The public continues to worship at the shrine of poets, short-story writers, playwrights, and novelists whom they consider to be the "creative" voices of our time. They fail to give enough adulation to the factual writer who also creates something from chaos. When you write an article, you take a shapeless mass of material and mold it into a form that will entertain or inform the reader. Shaping that article is every bit as creative as plotting a short story or working on the rhyme scheme of a sonnet. Articles are not made by stringing together facts and statistics. They require imagination and insight and they employ fiction techniques, such as dialogue and suspense.

Perhaps you dream of seeing your superb short story, quality essay, or unforgettable novel in *Saturday Evening Post, Reader's Digest, The Atlantic.* You may achieve that goal someday, but most writers put in an apprenticeship with lesser known publications before they start selling to top-notch markets. Many great authors first appeared in the pulps. Some article writers had their start writing for trade journals. You can earn from $25.00 to $500.00 for each article published in small magazines where competition is less keen, where editors work with you on revisions, and where the door is always open to unknown writers.

Structure of the Article

In general, there are two types of articles. One is the newspaper feature that starts off with a statement, followed by word pictures, incidents, and examples which illustrate the theme. The third part of the article includes minor details that are interesting, but which could be dropped from the article without ruining its sense. This news feature carries the Five W's in the first paragraph: Who, What, Why, When, Where. Less important material can be cut at the end in the interest of fitting the article into a limited space. Working on a newspaper is good training, regardless of what field of writing you hope to enter. You learn to gather facts, to check them for accuracy, and to present them in the most economical way. Hemingway worked as a newspaper reporter after he graduated from high-school. Edna Ferber started her career as a reporter on her hometown newspaper in Wisconsin. Other writers got their start working on school papers, community papers, or church bulletins.

In contrast to the news story, the most popular magazine article published today is the one that starts with a specific example or an illustrative incident. Following an anecdote are word pictures, incidents and examples expanding the theme. The article ends with a statement summarizing the main idea.

Once you have mastered the technique of writing articles based on this simple outline, you need no other. The framework can support any subject. For example, let's analyze the following article published in *Straight,* August 14, 1966:

EVERYONE HAS PROBLEMS

By Emalene Sherman

Part I Introduction. Theme implied.

A famous minister, author, and newspaper columnist recently said, "Problems are good for people because they are a sign of life. The more problems you have, the more alive you are. The only persons who do not have problems are in cemeteries."

Although we frequently associate problems with middle-aged and older persons, those who are realistic know that young people have worries too. Youth is synonymous with "having fun," but it is also a time when your body is developing at a rapid pace, your mind is expanding, and you are facing the task of eventually breaking away from your family and finding your own place in the world.

Part II

You are typical of your age group if you have problems in the following areas:

Example #1

1. *Acceptance of self.* No one is ever completely satisfied with his or her own looks. Tall persons want to be short. Brunettes wish they were blondes. Skinny teens would like to gain weight . . . The most common problem for both boys and girls during adolescence is skin eruptions. You have no doubt been told to follow a sensible diet (not too many soft drinks, chocolate, potato chips, etc.), and to get an adequate amount of sleep, fresh air, and exercise. If you are a girl and you are confused about what beauty preparations to use, consult someone whose judgment you trust—your mother, a favorite aunt, or a beautician. Boys can do little to cover up physical defects, but they can build up their bodies by following a regular program of athletics, weight-lifting, or exercise.

Remember three points in accepting yourself: (a)

There is only one you; you are unique, special, beloved by your family for your individuality. (b) You have inherited certain characteristics through genes that you cannot change; be glad for the good things and work to improve what you dislike. (c) Most problems that upset you now are a *temporary* condition; in time your skin will clear up, your voice will deepen, squeaks will disappear, your hair and body will respond to wise treatment.

Example #2

2. *Acceptance of others.* Some friends annoy you with excessive talking, giggling, punching, whistling. You will be bothered by others' habits and whims all your life. You have to learn to accept individuals for what they are, to accentuate the positive (their talents) and to eliminate the negative (their faults) in your thinking. You hope they do the same for you! Jesus looked beyond man's outward appearance into his soul, and you too, with practice, can see good in each person you meet. It is difficult to accept the opinions, instructions, and advice of your elders, especially parents. You cannot always agree with them, but you can tell yourself that since they have lived much longer than you, they have acquired some authority and wisdom. Love is the answer in dealing with all persons everywhere. Love accepts another's shortcomings and recognizes that none of us is perfect, even though we strive for godliness.

Example #3

3. *Personal faith.* When you were young you followed your parent's religion without question. As you mature and study about other religions, it is natural to go through a questioning period. If you have questions about religion and feel you do not care to discuss them with your parents, make an appointment to see your minister or a teacher in your Sunday school. Never try to solve your problems alone and avoid trying to work them out with someone your own age who might be just as confused as you are.

Example #4

4. *Boy-girl relationships.* You should date several persons before you settle down with one for life. In one

of Shakespeare's plays, Polonius advised his son, "To thine own self be true, and it must follow as the night the day that thou canst not then be false to any man." If your conscience tells you something is wrong, don't do it. It's better to be safe than sorry.

Example #5 5. *Your family*. Maybe you have a younger brother or sister who irritates you, or a father who is so busy talking about business that he has no time for discussing your questions, or a mother who appears to be more dedicated to meetings outside the home than to devoting time to you. Sometimes your parents are unaware that they are hurting you, just by failing to listen to your problems. Ask them to set aside an hour when you can talk in private, away from the rest of the family. They won't turn you down!

Example #6 6. *Conflict of standards*. When your circle of acquaintances widens through classrooms, clubs, part-time jobs, you will move beyond your church and family contacts into a world that could be bewildering if you let it. Your conscience can be stilled when you want to be a part of a group, or your better judgment can be overcome by wayward "friends." You can safeguard against these temptations by reading your Bible every day, going to church every Sunday, attending youth meetings, committing the Ten Commandments to memory. One girl learns a Bible verse of her own choosing every week and tucks it into her wallet to refer to when she feels torn in two directions. Be sure to memorize Philippians 4:13 and repeat it often to give you courage and assurance.

Part III Conclusion. Don't let your problems overwhelm you. Everybody has them. They are a necessary part of life. Anyone can solve a problem if he will think with his mind and not with his emotions.

Summation. He must learn too, to see God's guidance through prayer. This is the real secret of overcoming problems.

Notice that the author "goes out" where she "came in." The last paragraph repeats the thought in the title, that everyone has problems. In Part II, she expands the theme by giving six areas where most young people's problems lie. She appeals to you, the reader, by using the words "you" and "yours" in the examples. Part III summarizes the theme and offers a solution.

Whenever you read, look for the skeleton outline on which the writer has built her article. Whether it is long or short, profound or frothy, you will see that it follows a definite pattern. The more you work at writing, the easier it becomes for you to assemble your ideas into three distinct parts. The job is difficult at first, but it is clearer with practice. Your article must have a beginning, a middle, and an end.

A BEGINNING

(1) *Title.* The first words your reader sees are your title. It should catch his interest. It should give him a hint as to what the article is about. Use concrete, rather than vague words; try to make your title fresh and unusual. It should arouse the reader's curiosity and make him want to read on. It must be short and to the point. A good title helps to sell your manuscript to an editor, but if you have nothing of import to back it up, he will not buy the manuscript for the title alone. If the article is acceptable, but has a poor title, the editor will change it.

Titles fall into five classifications:

(a) Noun Title—"The Single Club"
(b) Question Title—"What Are You Doing New Year's Eve?"
(c) Statement Title—"It's Great to Be 40!"
(d) Quotation Title—"Do Unto Others . . ."
(e) The How, When, Why Title—"How to Start A Church Library" . . . "When You Are Blue . . ." or "Why You Need God"

(2) *Lead.* Your lead does just what the word implies: it leads your reader into your article. The first paragraph must either state the theme outright, or imply it. Your lead will fall into one of the following categories:

(a) *Newspeg*—"Twenty-five years ago today . . ."
(b) *Statement of purpose*—"Senior Citizens, this article will tell you how to look and feel younger."
(c) *Summary*—"Life in suburbia is full of sounds: the barking of dogs, the screams of children, the hum of power lawn mowers."
(d) *Epigram*—"If you believe that life is a bowl of cherries, be sure they are ripe before you start picking them."
(e) *Direct Address*—"Madame, your quips are showing."
(f) *Striking Statement*—"One out of four marriages ends in divorce."
(g) *Question*—"Is television ruining our reading habits?"
(h) *Anecdote*—"One evening last April, my sister left home without a word to anyone."
(i) *Narrative*—"A school bus driver stopped the bus and told his passengers that if they did not quiet down, they would have to walk home."
(j) *Description*—"She was a five-year-old pixie eating an orange when I first saw her."

Your subject matter, and to some extent, your own personality, determine how you will start your article, but remember that the anecdote is an easy way to begin. You are almost certain of catching your reader's attention at the outset if you use a short fictionalized beginning.

A Middle

My mother always said that if she had promised me something, I'd get it, even if it was a whipping. And she followed through on her promise. The middle of your article gives your reader what you promised him in the beginning. You told him what you were going to do, if not in so many words, at least by implication, and now you do it. To accomplish your aim, you use words, sentences and paragraphs.

(1) *Words.* The words you use stem from your education, family background, associations, the amount of reading you do, and a great many other factors. You have a feeling for words,

a sense of how to put them together effectively, or you would not be reading this book. When you write:

(a) Make sure that the words you use are correct. Refer to your dictionary if you are not sure of spelling or meaning.

(b) Avoid words and phrases that are obsolete. (*Hath* for *has,* or *wend* for *go*).

(c) Avoid slang. If you hope to write for posterity, stay away from slang, for these expressions eventually lose their punch because people no longer know what is meant by them. Some examples are: corny, grub, phony, savvy, scram.

(d) Choose words that are clear in meaning.

(e) Choose words that are colorful and vivid, not colorless or commonplace.

(f) Use the specific or concrete word instead of the general or abstract. General words name classes or groups (bird, tree, insect). Specific words name members of a group (robin, oak, beetle).

(g) Use verbs of descriptive action ("tramped" instead of "walked").

(h) Avoid trite expressions. (After all is said and done . . . goes without saying . . . in all its glory . . . riot of color).

(i) Use figures of speech.

(j) Write naturally and sincerely.

(k) Write compactly.

Mark Twain said, "I never write 'metropolis' for seven cents when I can get the same price for 'city.' "

(2) *Sentences.* A sentence may consist of a few parts or of many; it is simple, complex, or compound. The words must form a single organic whole that clearly expresses a complete meaning. Each sentence must have (a) a subject, about which something is said, and (b) a predicate, which says something about the subject. Lively writing comes from varying the length of your sentences. You learn through practice to keep some of them short and a few of them long. In informal writing it is all right to use the incomplete sentence in conversation, as well as contractions. You do not use contractions in formal writing,

but you do use them for natural speech. Use *I'll go* instead of *I shall go* when a person is speaking.

(3) *Paragraphs.* The paragraph is the smallest unit of writing that can be called a composition. It is usually part of a larger structure, but it can stand alone and it often does, as a brief feature article in popular magazines. The word *paragraph* comes from two Greek words and means literally *written beside.* Several sentences on the same subject are written together as a visual unit and separated from the rest of the theme by indention. When the reader sees indention, he knows that you are going to present a new idea. Paragraphs help to break up print on a page and make it easier to read than if it were solid writing with no indention at all.

Within the paragraph there must be three qualities:

(1) *Unity or oneness.* All the sentences are related statements about one idea or thing or action. Start with a topic sentence and relate other sentences to it. In the article on problems, for example, here is a topic sentence: "Although we frequently associate problems with middle-aged and older persons, those who are realistic know that young people have worries too." The sentences that follow enlarge on that idea.

(2) *Coherence* or "sticking together of like substances." Some ideas are more closely related to your subject than others. You can achieve coherence by using verbal links and by the orderly arrangement of ideas. Verbal links are: (a) pronouns referring to something in the preceding sentence, (b) repetition of words or ideas from a preceding section, and (c) transition words and phrases: *but, on the other hand, moreover, later,* and others. When you have been writing for some time, these transitions will come to you without your thinking too much about them. You will automatically sort out your thoughts and put them in proper order. Practice writing paragraphs and you will soon select the pattern that best suits your purpose.

(3) *Complete development.* A paragraph which is completely developed is one that unfolds or reveals a complete idea. Many times we are so enthusiastic about our subject and it is so well

known to us that we leave out points we think we are putting across to the reader. When someone reads what we have written, he says, "I'm not sure what you mean." Read your paragraphs aloud. Try to hear them as someone else would. This is not easy. For this very reason, you should put your writing away for a few days before rewriting it, so that when you get it out again you can see it with new eyes, hear it with new ears. You can develop ideas by:

Description. Tell how something looks, feels, smells, tastes, sounds.
Examples.
Comparison (point out similarities or differences)
Definition (taken from the dictionary)
Repetition

Check your paragraphs by asking yourself: can I state the topic in one sentence? Do my paragraphs have unity, coherence, and complete development? If they meet those requirements, you are ready to finish the whole composition.

Every composition has form, substance, meaning, style. Your article is not merely a collection of paragraphs; the paragraphs glide smoothly into each other and each separate unit contributes toward the whole. The finished article must have the same qualities as the individual paragraphs: unity, organization, completeness. To these points you add interest. What makes your work interesting to others? You do. When you are choosing a subject, bear in mind the eternal concerns of man: himself, his income, health, safety, sex, love, marriage, children, patriotism, politics, aesthetic inspiration, religion. Your specific touch gives new life to old topics.

The End

Always try to tie up your ending with the beginning. Just by repeating a word or two in the last sentence that you used in the first one, or in the title, you give your composition a wholeness, a completeness that is satisfying to the reader. (Study again the article, "Everyone Has Problems.")

Endings should leave the reader with something to remember. You yourself know that you read so much that you cannot possibly retain everything. Words and sentences have a way of sliding into your unconscious mind and although you gain general knowledge from reading, you have difficulty with specific facts. *If*, however, you read an article that ends with a snappy quotation, a practical idea, or an incident amusingly told, you will remember it long after you have laid the magazine aside.

The last sentence of your article should be a summing up of the theme in your own original way.

Chapter IV

YOUR MANUSCRIPT

And, after all, it is style alone by which posterity will judge of a great work, for an author can have nothing truly his own but his style.

—ISAAC D'ISRAELI

Why is it that if two people use the same ingredients in a cake, one turns out a failure and the other produces a culinary delight? We say vaguely that one lacked a certain something; he brought no imagination to his work. The other has a talent for cooking. He is gifted. Male cooks often excel over women in the kitchen because they dare to be different; a pinch of this and a dash of that add zing to their dishes. What is true for cooking is also true for article writing. Given a set of ingredients, no two writers will turn out the same result.

STYLE

Style has been called "a way with words," "the dress of thought," "the flavor of writing, its quality and spirit," and "the man himself."

Two facts you can be sure of: your style is distinctly yours (even though you are unaware of it) and it will improve as you write, just as your cooking improves with practice. The biggest reward for a writer, aside from finding a check in his mailbox, is to hear someone say, "I knew it was your work. I recognized your style."

If you feel that you need to review the rules of grammar, ask your librarian or bookseller to recommend a good composition book. If you have not already read *The Elements of Style* by William Strunk, Jr., be sure to get a copy.

Another place to learn about style is from the magazines for which you are trying to write. Do they use homey phrases or erudite expressions? Do they appeal to the average person, or are they slanted toward the egghead? The tone of the articles the editors have already bought is your key as to how to develop your own writing.

Editors usually prefer to buy the simple, clear, concise article, instead of a complicated, flowery, rambling jungle of words. Writing of this kind is achieved only by laborious rewriting, striking out pompous phrases, eliminating every unnecessary word.

In writing about "Shirt-Sleeve English in One Easy Lesson," Rudolf Flesch gave the following rules:

1. Go slow on rare and fancy words.
2. Don't worry too much about avoiding repetition.
3. Don't worry too much about avoiding slang.
4. Don't worry too much about being grammatical.

He went on to say:

> For effective speaking and writing, simple words are better than fancy ones. Somerset Maugham says proudly, "The nicest compliment ever paid me came from a GI in the Pacific who wrote that he had read an entire story of mine without having to look up a single word in the dictionary."
>
> People often fall back on fancy words because they are afraid to repeat a simple word. Here's an example—the first sentence of a book on modern civilization: "The state of mind following the recent war differs from that subsequent to the previous one." No doubt what the professor had in mind was, "The state of mind after this war is different than it was after the last war."
>
> Maybe your schoolteacher warned you against repetition in the use of the word "said" in written dialogue. But Scott, Cooper, Poe and O. Henry all used "said" more often than any substitute. So

if you find you've used the same word twice in a sentence, relax. Chances are it was the best word in both places.*

Read great writers of the past and absorb their style. (Remember Hemingway's hard-hitting conversation in *The Killers*?) Read textbooks pointing the way toward developing an acceptable style. Then shove these ideas deep into your subconscious and proceed to write in your own inimitable way. In general, the best style comes from the use of:

1. Simple words.
2. Short, uninvolved sentences.
3. Figures of speech used sparingly.
4. Compactness.
5. A personal tone.

Experts can tell you what goes into an article, but you learn short-cuts only by working at it yourself. You learn to bake by rolling up your sleeves and doing the job on your own.

Your Recipe

Every cook has a file of recipes that she refers to over and over again. She usually has a specialty, a dish that she is famous for among her friends. Thousands of tried-and-true recipes appear in books and magazines, but although she follows them occasionally, she returns to the ones her family enjoys and the ones she knows cannot fail.

Here is a recipe that repeatedly works for any kind of an article:

(1) *Sift dry ingredients.* In any article, there are certain basic facts that you want to put across to the reader. Some of the material you dig out of encyclopedias is dry. Choose the facts that are most important to your end-product and discard the others. Type your notes with their source. Typing helps to fix them in your mind.

* *Printer's Ink,* June 30, '50, © 1950 by Decker Communications, Inc., 501 Madison Ave., New York, N.Y. 10022.

(2) *Measure all ingredients.* Type a rough outline, covering what you want to say, along with any quotes from persons you might have interviewed. Choose an angle, a point of view. Decide where to use facts and statistics. After you have a mental picture of how the article is going to shape up, let it rest. Don't return to it until at least twenty-four hours have passed.

(3) *Mix the batter, alternating dry and liquid ingredients.* Your article begins to take form when you gently stir quotes, facts, anecdotes into dry background material. Work with a light touch. At this point, your style determines the outcome of your article.

(4) *Pour mixture into a mold.* After you have baked your ideas, after they have been molded together by heat, they must hold their shape before a publisher's discerning eyes. If you have used a "mix" for a quickie article, he sends it back, but if you have started from "scratch" and have done a professional-like job, he sends you a check.

Manuscript Form

When you are satisfied that your manuscript is the very best you can produce, send it off to an editor and forget about it. Get busy on something else. Here is a brief summary of rules for preparing a manuscript for marketing:

1. Type the manuscript, double-spaced.
2. Use wide margins.
3. Write only on one side of the page.
4. On each page, in the upper left-hand corner, type the title of the manuscript, your name, and page number. For example:
   "Be Glad You're Sixteen!"—Doe—p.2
5. Write *more* at the bottom of each page and *30* or # at the end of the article.
6. Use a cover page. Some writers do not do this, but a cover page does keep a manuscript clean and gives it a professional appearance. It carries a statement that you expect to be paid at the regular rates of the magazine. Example:

(Sample Cover Page)

To be paid for at your usual rates, or returned in enclosed stamped envelope to: Approx.———words

Name
Street Address
City, State, Zip Code

(TITLE)
by
(name)

7. Do *not* send a letter with the manuscript. If you feel it is necessary to give credit for source material, you can put a notation underneath your name on the cover page. For example: *Note: The quote on p. 2 was taken from* Bartlett's Quotations, *p. 3. This article was based on an interview with Dr. Chester Blank, and he has read and approved it.*
8. Mail your manuscript flat and enclose postage and a self-addressed envelope for its return. If it is five pages or less, you can fold it and mail it in a #10 white envelope; otherwise, use the manuscript-size manila envelope.
9. File your carbon copy. Never send out a manuscript without keeping a copy. Although mail service and editors are generally reliable, manuscripts do get lost. I keep carbons in a large envelope, the kind you buy in the ten-cent store, with a string to tie it. After an article has been sold, I take the copy out of the envelope and put it in a folder marked, *Mss. Sold—196—,* with a notation as to the amount of money it earned for me, the letter of acceptance, and other pertinent information.

As I mentioned in Chapter III, I keep a list of manuscripts "Pending" in my card file. When an article has been sold, I simply move the card to the *Sold* division. This method makes it easy to total entire sales at the end of the year for income-tax purposes.

A typical card on a manuscript looks like this:

HOW TO START A CHURCH LIBRARY

Magazine	*Date Sent*	*Result*
Ace Pubs.	Dec. 12, 1961	R
Christian Advocate	Jan. 1, 1962	R
The Lookout	Jan. 17, 1962	Sold: $25

In addition to keeping a record of the money you earn, list expenditures: typewriter ribbons, postage, typing paper, and envelopes. When you make out your income tax, other legitimate deductions are: subscriptions to writers' magazines; subscriptions to newspapers and magazines used in free-lance writing; the purchase price of books of reference used in gathering information for your business, because writing *is* a business. If you employ an agent, you may also include his fees, and you may deduct depreciation of your typewriter. Check with your Internal Revenue Service Center for current rules. Personally, I feel that I do not need the services of an agent for the kind of writing I do; if an article is good, it will sell. Once I have sold to an editor, repeated sales are easy if I am able to continue to slant material toward his market.

Copyright

Your own unpublished manuscript is your exclusive property. You usually need not worry about having it copyrighted, for it probably will be copyrighted when it is published in a magazine. Look in the front of most magazines and you will see the copyright sign © in small print, followed by the year and the name of the publishing company.

What about using information that is already in print? You may take notes freely in your own words from reference books because *facts* cannot be copyrighted. Never copy the exact words, however, unless you intend to give credit as to book, author, publisher, date of publication, and page number. Also, permission may be required for a direct quote.

Suppose you are attending a meeting and you would like to quote the speaker. To be on the safe side, I would get the speaker's O.K. on my manuscript before submitting it to a publisher. He could sue me if I misquoted him! One way that the editor will know that your source is agreeable to the quotes you use is for you to include a page such as this:

To whom it may concern:

I have read this manuscript and I approve the use of the quotations on pp.____________________

____

(Signed)

You may quote freely from historical and public documents. As for letters, diaries, and historical records, these are almost certain not to be copyrighted, but you need permission since they are private property. You may quote from works on which the copyright law has expired. Under current law, it is in effect for 28 years and can be renewed for 28 more years. Suppose you are merely restating a person's opinions from a printed source? It is best to credit the source. If you use a direct quotation of less than fifty words, properly credited, the publisher will usually permit its use. If you want to quote more than fifty words, write to the owner of the copyright for permission.

The United States government publishes several circulars relating to copyright. To obtain information about them, write to: Copyright Office, Washington, D.C., 20025.

Freelance Writer's Code

The National Writers' Club, 745 Sherman Street, Denver, Colorado 80203, has prepared The Freelance Writer's Standard of Practice. Whatever you write, these rules are good ones to follow:

1. I will always carefully check and verify all facts used, whether in fiction or in articles.
2. I will revise carefully to correct any errors in spelling, punctuation or grammar that may be present.

3. Recognizing that I am offering something to be sold to a market that has professional standards, I will make sure before submitting any ms. that it is written interestingly and is about a subject worth reading. (Check with unbiased friends or a professional critic.)
4. My script will always be professionally prepared: clean type, dark ribbon, ample margins all around, name and address in upper left-hand corner, double spacing throughout, an over-all neat appearance.
5. Before submitting any manuscript to a magazine, I will learn as much as I can of its requirements, slant and readership. Of course, this applies to fiction as well as to other forms.
6. *Never will I send out a ms. in a vain hope that it just might sell though it fails to subscribe to all the foregoing points.*
7. With each submission I will send an addressed, stamped envelope, not merely loose postage.
8. At no time will I ask an editor to criticize or comment on a submitted ms., or will I argue with any comment volunteered by him. If the editor has misunderstood or erred, I will politely point this out only if in so doing my ms. then may prove acceptable to him.
9. I will not become unduly impatient for a report on my ms. or trouble an editor with unnecessary correspondence of any kind.

CODE OF ETHICS

1. At no time will I knowingly use the ideas or material of others without giving proper credit where required.
2. I will always do my utmost to use and interpret facts accurately. I will not misquote, use statements out of context, or misrepresent.
3. When asked to do a re-write or revision, I will do so promptly and to the best of my ability. If a request contrary to my convictions is made, I will refuse politely. When given an assignment, I will carry it out immediately. Should this be impossible, I will notify the editor at once.
4. Never will I use my writing to the disadvantage of my country, the ideals of religion, democracy and decency.
5. I will always strive for better workmanship and to be a credit

> to freelance writers. I know that the desirable freelance system may be endangered by carelessness and indifference to editorial and freelance standards.

Once you have dropped your manuscript in the mail, get to work on another one without delay. Do not haunt the mailbox, because you will not get a check or a rejection slip tomorrow, or even the next day. Weeks may pass before you know the outcome. You cannot afford to waste them in wishful thinking. Forgetting those things which are behind, you must ever press on toward your goal: publication of your work.

Chapter V

WHERE TO SELL IT

No man but a blockhead ever wrote except for money.

—SAMUEL JOHNSON

Above my typewriter I have a cartoon on the wall. The scene is a party. A talkative woman is seated on a couch beside a bespectacled man. "I'm so thrilled to meet an author," she gushes. "What do you do for a living?"

Her attitude is prevalent today among nonwriters and aspiring writers. They do not consider writing to be work; in their minds, an author is an artistic fellow who dashes off "a piece" when he is "inspired." He joyously writes "off the top of his head" and then he attends cocktail parties, collects royalties, and signs autographs.

Successful writers simply have very little time for such activities. They sit at the typewriter or with a pad and pencil in hand every day whether they feel inspired or not. They suffer aching muscles . . . leg cramps . . . tired fingers . . . rumpled hair . . . flagging spirits. They drink endless cups of coffee or consume bottles of soft drinks. They walk the floor and talk to themselves. Thousands of them make a living this way. Thousands of others supplement their regular income by writing on a free-lance basis.

If you are a beginner, you have a tendency to write for self-expression. At first you are too shy to expose your work to the eyes of another. You pour out your secret longings, hopes, and frustrations on paper and then hide the stacks of sheets in a drawer. Such writing is excellent practice, but as you gain in knowledge and experience you will want to see your work in print. You should be paid for your time, because there is no more demanding task physically and mentally than writing.

By far the most exciting part of this business is marketing. Who will pay you for your work? Since you cannot possibly see all the magazines published in one month, you should subscribe to at least one *writer's magazine* to learn what editors require. The top three publish market lists covering all types of publications: general magazines, home service and women's magazines, men's publications, the confessions, fact detective, fictional detective and mystery, science fiction, fantasy, business magazines, travel, religious, juvenile publications. They also give the address of the editorial offices, name of the editor, word length used, type of material, and rate of payment. They feature tips to writers, interviews with editors, and articles on all phases of writing and marketing. The only way you can keep in touch with the publishing business, especially if you work at home, is to read regularly one of the following:

Author & Journalist, published monthly at National Press Building, Washington, D.C., 20004. The subscription price is $5.00 for one year, $9.00 for two years, and $12.00 for three years. Single copies sell for 50¢, but you might not be able to find it on your newsstand. Several magazines are discontinued every year and new ones appear. Market lists go out of date. This magazine is valuable to the writer because it carries market lists covering many magazines and their requirements.

Writer's Digest, published monthly at 22 East 12th Street, Cincinnati, Ohio, 45210. The subscription rate is $4.00 per year, $7.50 for two years. Single copies are 50¢. (*The Writer's Yearbook,* published by *Writer's Digest,* comes out every Spring and it is well worth $1.25. It carries several market lists, including the "100 Best Markets," as well as other information for writers. Another valuable source is their *Writer's Market,* which sells for $7.50.)

The Writer, published monthly at 8 Arlington Street, Boston, Mass. Same price as other writers' magazines.

You will find many helpful books on writing advertised in these magazines, but do not spend too much time reading or you will not have time to write.

Second-Class Markets

In choosing a market, you are wise to start with second-class magazines until you have established a name for yourself. You dislike that idea, don't you? I did, too, at first. We Americans want first-class accommodations in everything. We want the best, to be on top, and yet we laud the man who starts at the bottom in business and works his way up.

I work with several market lists beside my typewriter. I feel that referring to some of them as "second class" is a misnomer. These magazines often publish superior writing. Do not be embarrassed when friends ask you, "What magazines are you published in? *Reader's Digest? Good Housekeeping? Life?*" You can try those magazines once in a while, but you will discover, as I did, that they buy very little free-lance material. Sometimes my friends are puzzled when I mention magazines they never heard of, some of which are not even sold in our town, but I explain to them that I find the names of these magazines in market lists, and they add this bit of knowledge to their own list of reasons why writers are odd.

If you are writing for money (and eventual prestige), you gain several rewards from selling your material to lesser known publications:

1. *You receive a steady income of small checks.* My records show that over a period of six months I earned $609.20 free-lancing. You can increase that amount if you are able to spend more time writing than I did, and if your ideas click more often than mine. Some magazines pay on acceptance, some on publication. I would rather get a small check every month than a big one once a year!

2. *You see your articles in print.* If what you write is not quite good enough for top markets, you might be tempted to give up writing. Don't! They could make the grade in smaller

publications. Rather than sticking rejected manuscripts out of sight, you can reach an audience through magazines of limited circulation.

3. *You are building a name for yourself.* After several submissions, you can be sure that editors are beginning to recognize your work. If they cannot use your material, they often write an encouraging letter, recommending other markets.

4. *You mature in writing ability.* You learn to write only by writing. When you are aiming toward a specific market, you strive to do your very best. Each time you work on a manuscript, you improve your style.

5. *You often receive free copies of the magazine in which your work appears.* Most of these editors send you marked copies of the magazine carrying your article. One editor sends me six copies. It is gratifying to be able to pass on extra copies to relatives and friends, and it is rewarding to know that the persons closest to you will have an opportunity to read your work that they might otherwise miss if they had to watch for it on the newsstands.

6. *Your faith is lifted.* Writers are sensitive, withdrawn, moody. We slide into the dumps easier than most people do. If an editor accepts our work, we scurry back to the typewriter, but if he rejects it, we tend to brood about our shortcomings and to tell ourselves that we are not writers after all. Your work gets a more thorough, honest evaluation on the desk of a man who has fifty manuscripts to read than it does on the desk of a reader who can scarcely see above the 500 manuscripts piled in front of him.

Following is a brief description of five types of magazines where your work will most likely find a home:

Religious Magazines

At this writing, more than eighty religious magazines are published in this country. They are either Sunday school papers distributed in classes according to age groups, or the home-service magazine usually sold by subscription and offering the entire family entertaining and informative reading. Chances are you read at least one of them each month.

You will be most successful in trying to sell your writing if you submit material to the publication you are familiar with; but, whether you are Catholic, Jewish, or Protestant, you can sell to magazines of any denomination if your material is right for their slant. Every church leader realizes the importance of its young people, for they are the church of tomorrow. You will find a welcome in the religious editor's office.

You know better than anyone else what interests youth; you see these topics appearing again and again in church papers: cars, driving lessons, camping, dating, sports (especially top-notch performance by athletes who have a deep religious belief), personal matters involving self-discipline, getting along with others, having a goal in life and how to work toward it. But you need not limit yourself to writing about young people. Perhaps your minister took a trip to the Holy Land. Interview him about his vacation. Ask him if he has any glossy pictures you could use to illustrate an article. Does your church have a library? Tell others how to start one in their church. Is there a devoted prayer group that meets weekly, a new kind of music being used by your choir, an outstanding woman's society program in your church? All of these activities could be turned into articles. Maybe someone in your congregation has an unusual Bible, a rare scroll, or ancient religious books. Perhaps a family you know conducts a daily family worship service. Has someone in your church experienced a miraculous healing? His story could be an inspiration to others. When dealing with material of this nature, it is a good idea to have the interviewee's o.k. on the manuscript before you mail it to an editor. Ask your minister to read it, too; he might want to correct some minor point about theology that you overlooked.

As you do with all magazines before submitting your work to them, study the religious publications. They do not carry stuffy, dull, encyclopedia fare. Far from it! Editors strive to please their readers with lively, up-to-the minute pieces on many subjects: homemaking, hobbies, child care, travelogues, as well as inspirational themes. There are certain topics that are often taboo if presented in a favorable light: crime, war, divorce, dancing, gambling, bazaars, theatres, movies. While religious magazines steer away from such topics, one recently published an article on how one should treat her divorced friends. They frequently contain a discussion on alcoholism and its affect on the family. They do not close their eyes to the existence of evil; they will print articles about sins as long as they are not presented favorably. In Catholic magazines the subject matter need not be exclusively Catholic, but viewpoints in contradiction to Catholic teaching are obviously unacceptable.

The word "quality" applies to all writing for religious magazines. Do not think you can dash off an article and sell it to them if it will not fit in anywhere else. Take your time. Think your subject through. Do just as good work as you would on a story for the slicks. Although the pay is small, you might collect two checks, for *Reader's Digest* often reprints articles from religious magazines.

Some of the religious magazines send free tips to writers. One is *Power,* published by Scripture Press Foundation, 1825 College Avenue, Wheaton, Illinois. Churches of over 50 denominations distribute these church papers; there is an edition for teenagers and one for adults. They contain fiction, short features, fillers, and nonfiction under the general headings: real-life profiles, biographical sketches, "It Happened To Me" accounts, and special adult features, such as human-interest articles dealing with the Christian and his problems and activities at home, at work, and at church. The editors, who also publish *Counselor,* a paper read by boys and girls nine to twelve years old, will send you their twelve-page booklet for writers, free on request.

Another publishing house that sends out an informative pamphlet for the writer is Christian Publications, Inc., Third and Reilly Streets, Harrisburg, Pennsylvania. It publishes *Council*

Fires, an 8-page weekly paper intended for high-school and college-age readers. *Christian Trails,* another 8-page weekly paper, is aimed at junior and intermediate-age readers. Stories must have some definite Christian lesson or message, but should avoid preaching. The editors buy Biblical crossword puzzles and quizzes. Seasonal material must be submitted nine months in advance.

Home Life is typical of the home-service type religious publication. Here is what they consider suitable topics for free-lancers to work on:

Activity—anything that brings the family together for wholesome fun, work, or cultural development, such as: gardening, hobbies, vacation, home movies, eating, visitors in the home, family council, playroom, workroom, improving the attic, reading, singing.

Housing—always a subject of live interest to every family. Timely or special features on the housing problem would be of great value.

Adoption—feature stories on homes that have adopted children, legal aspects, psychological and religious problems, a cure for mental and social ills.

Anecdotes—"It Happened at Our House," short stories on family life.

Features—full-length human interest pen pictures of homes that are successfully Christian. Preferably ordinary homes. A well-known family might be used infrequently. A human interest story of a normal, obscure Christian family is carried in each issue, about 2,000–3,000 words.

Worship—human interest articles focusing on the family worshipping at home or at church. The home co-operating with the church in cultivating a spirit of worship. The child developing in worship.

Doctrine—"I married a Presbyterian, or a Methodist, or a Catholic, a Christian Scientist, a non-Christian." Interfaith marriage and the problem it poses treated from the viewpoint of personal experience. Features on couples who found the answer —it should, of course, be a positive, Christian answer, one that does no violence to personality, to faith, or to the truth of God's Word. There should also be other material on doctrine as it relates to home life. For instance, one home has a weekly session, requested by the children, on Baptist beliefs.

Missions—the home cultivating an interest in missions, growing an atmosphere from which young people will be called to world service for Christ. A reporter's story based on interview or observation or both.

Children—taking their place in the family, developing toward maturity. Anything on the home's influence on child life.

Special Problems—the afflicted child. Two families brought together by a second marriage. Apartment house living. Urban life. Rural homes. Neighborhood annoyances. Delinquency. Threats to the home (liquor, divorce, immorality).

Education—kindergarten, good or bad? The home cooperating with the public school. College for my child: parents stimulating a will to go, meeting expenses, adjusting to the home separation. College marriage, good or bad? Books in the home. Childhood training in the home.

Finances—achieving a balance (both emotionally and on the ledger). Features that focus on the scriptural attitude toward substance.

Institutions—those that affect home life: school, church, movies, newspapers, comics, summer camps, advertising (billboard and publication), radio, TV, clubs, commercial entertainment. Manuscripts that help to evaluate these institutions and make proper use of them are needed. Both indirect and direct treatment could be used.

Visitation—the church planning and executing a home visitation program. Why visit? How? What should the religious visitor do in the home?

The magazine also contains:

Cartoons—a drawing and a line of copy which say something forcefully, pointedly, wittily on family life.

Puzzles and quizzes—with family angle.

Poetry—inspirational, seasonal, child life, family setting.

Fiction—wholesome stories with a message on any phase of family living.

Photos—pictures of life in the home, good technically, showing meaningful activity.

JUVENILES

You no doubt read some of the juvenile publications, either because you subscribe to them for your own pleasure, or because you read them to your brothers and sisters. They fall into three groups:

(1) *Youth.* At present, thirteen youth magazines are published. The ones slanted toward girls, such as *The American Girl,* use articles on hobbies, current events, sports, music, homemaking, careers, dating, international friendship, crafts, school, parties, and other subjects of interest to teenagers. They also publish short stories and serials for ages ten to sixteen. *Boy's Life* and similar magazines for boys use space, foreign background, mystery, outdoor adventure, and special holiday fiction. Articles are wanted on science and vocational guidance slanted toward boys in high school, as well as short stories about animals and nature. Of course, it is best to look at several recent issues of any magazine you wish to submit material to, because sometimes they are overstocked on certain topics.

(2) *Younger Readers.* Magazines in this group are slanted roughly toward the eight- to thirteen-year-olds. Interests in fiction are suspense, excitement dealing with school life, beginning boy-girl situation, sports, history, science, humor and animals. Nonfiction leans toward science, hobbies, good looks and how to get along with others.

(3) *Religious.* The subject matter here is practically the same, with a little more emphasis on nature, hobbies and Christian service. Twenty-one magazines are aimed at early teens, the ten- to fifteen-year-olds. For the ages from nine to twelve there are

nineteen publications; for the four- to nine-year-olds there are thirteen magazines. Stories are needed on three grade levels: 1, 2 and 3. If you are adept at riddles, puzzles, special day articles, plays, and how to make things, you have a ready market here. You are best suited for writing for this age group if you have a younger brother or sister, because you can tell what appeals to him, and you can read some of his books and papers to get an idea of how to slant your writing toward this age group.

Travel

Whether you take a trip to another state or to a foreign land, or if you just stay at home next summer, you will be exposed to enough travel ideas to pay for your vacation.

Do you have younger brothers and sisters? If you have ever taken a car trip with them, you know how restless they become after a few hours' driving. Maybe you have devised several games to keep them busy. One of them is seeing who can spot license plates from the greatest number of states. Maybe you "collect" road signs or different kinds of trees and flowers; perhaps you make a game of checking places on the map, or keeping a log of all the towns you pass through and the mileage you cover. You can use such material for an article on travel tips for parents and submit it to women's magazines or baby publications.

For travel magazines, write about places you visit. They use articles about off-beat or well-known tourist objectives. The editorial requirement sheet from *Motor News* gives a good summary of what travel articles should be:

> In addition to descriptions of things to see and do, articles should contain accurate, current information on costs the traveler would encounter on his trip. Items such as lodging, meal and entertainment expenses should be included, not in the form of a balance sheet but as an integral part of the article. Tips on what to pack and wear and other trip planning features should be included.
>
> Our readers want articles that verbally transport them to the

area being described. They want to know what they should do and see, as well as what they should avoid. On the strength of the article alone, they should be able to decide whether or not they would enjoy visiting the area in person some day. Both good and bad points, if any, should be mentioned.

In addition to pieces on actual locations in the United States, we also are interested in "things to do" subjects concerning camping, hunting, fishing, boating and special events. We are always in the market for pieces about Michigan.

Some travel magazines cover one area exclusively; others use material about all states and some carry articles on foreign countries.

When you travel, make notes. Buy picture postcards wherever you see them. Collect travel folders. Talk to caretakers and guides. Take pictures. Good glossy photos help to sell the travel article. If you are not a camera fan, maybe your father or another member of your family can click the shutter for you. Sometimes you can buy glossy prints in a gift shop where you visit. If you interview someone, ask him if he has pictures that you might borrow or buy from him. A small magazine or newspaper occasionally accepts stock photos obtained from a chamber of commerce or a state travel bureau. Color shots are increasing in demand. The most acceptable size is 4x5 or larger, but some art directors will consider pictures as small as 3¼x3¼. Black and white glossies should be 8½x11.

As soon as you have some free time (perhaps even while you are still riding in the car), outline your article. When you get home, go to the library and check the *Reader's Guide* to see if anything has been published on your subject within the last year. If there has been a big spread in a national magazine, your idea is temporarily dead. But do not toss your preliminary work into the wastebasket! File it for future use. You can always dig it out in a year or two and give it a new angle. A query letter might save you time, because many travel articles are assigned. Tell the editor your approximate word length and how many pictures you have. If he is interested in your idea, get to work immediately and send him the finished product promptly, within a week if you can. Use stiff cardboard on each side of your pictures. This will run up your postage bill, but your pictures will not be crumpled in transit. Write your name and address on the back of them *lightly* in pencil—and give a credit line to the photographer, if someone other than yourself has taken the photo.

It is not easy to see article ideas in familiar surroundings, but they are there if you look for them. In your hometown you might take for granted a spot that others travel miles to see: a new planetarium, your city's zoo, a monument to a famous person in your town park. If you live in a small town or in a rural area, there might be a fisherman's paradise near you, or a mountain retreat, or a state park. In scouting around for places to visit, you could come across material for an article that would sell to *Field & Stream, Sports Afield,* or *Outdoor Life*. Besides gathering material for travel magazines, you could turn your notes into a feature for boating magazines, men's magazines, regional outdoor magazines, or the general slicks. Fishermen, hunters, and boat owners like to read articles that are technically correct and written with authority. They are not travel articles in the strict sense of the word, but they could inspire someone to travel to a spot he has never visited before, just to try out his new fishing lure or his new boat. As a rule, technical articles on tackle, guns, and the technique of using them are staff-written or written by old pros of long standing. The easiest pieces for you to sell are the how-to-do-it picture story and the where-to-go travel story. Rates vary from 1¢ to 5¢ per word, with extra payment for pictures, usually $3 or $5 each.

Do not forget about newspapers and general magazines when you are writing about places to visit. For example, a Sunday school paper might use an article on the Gingerbread Castle in Hamburg, New Jersey, or Daniel Boone's Home in Defiance, Missouri, or President Ulysses S. Grant's home in Pt. Pleasant, Ohio. Sunday supplements carry travel articles. It is possible to write about the same place in two different ways and sell one article to a travel magazine and the other to another type of publication. They would have to be two entirely different articles, however; *never* submit the same article to two magazines at the same time.

Trade Journals

Do you enjoy interviewing people? If so, you should explore the trade journal field, a lucrative source of income for a writer who is not afraid of leg work and who likes to deal with businessmen and facts. Over 150 trade and business magazines are published on such topics as aviation, banks, boats, glass, poultry, flowers, fur, furniture, groceries, etc. Every businessman is interested in finding out how to solve problems in his line and how to increase his profits.

Your articles should contain step-by-step information on how the reader can increase productivity, build sales, or cut operating costs. Action photographs help to sell it, and if pertinent to your story, you might want to include charts or graphs. Business experience in a field is helpful. If your father runs a particular business, you might get all the information you need from him, plus reference books and pamphlets on the topic. Some articles, however, are based entirely on interviews, and if there is some point you are not sure of, you can always go back to the businessman and check it with him. In fact, it is a good idea to ask him to read the article anyway, before you submit it to a magazine, so that he cannot accuse you later of distorting facts or leaving out important points.

Be sure to study the trade journal before sending in material. Many large libraries have a business section with a rack displaying a variety of such magazines. Maybe the person you interview can give you a few back copies of the magazine in his particular trade. If these two sources fail, write to the editors of trade magazines you hope to sell to, and ask them for a sample copy. For names and addresses, consult a trade journal list in a writers' magazine, or one of the following in your library:

N. W. Ayer and Son's *Directory of Newspapers and Periodicals*

Annual Market Data & Directory Number of Industrial Marketing Magazine

Writing for specialized magazines, as for the business journals, demands accuracy. The specialized publications cover Amusements, Armed Forces, the Arts, Astrology, Crafts, Mechanics, Hobbies, Education, Health and Personal Improvement, Humor, Nature and Science, Pets, Photography, Picture Magazines, Regional Magazines, Sports and Recreation. These magazines have small circulations and the people who read them are well versed on the subject matter. You might want to try the specialized market with articles on yachting, antiques, or hobbies—any topic that you have a great deal of background information on because you have made a special study of it, or because you have collected items in that category for several years.

Specialized publications number over one hundred. The difference between them and the business magazines is their purpose. A business magazine is definitely specialized, but it goes to readers who earn their livelihood from the occupations reported upon: running motels, building bridges, selling groceries. The specialized magazine is aimed at people whose interest in the subject is a matter of personal improvement, public service, or recreation. Both have been called "the market that works with you," for editors are patient and helpful. Some of them advertise in writers' magazines for correspondents in certain cities, and if you are the type of writer who can produce readable material within a deadline date, you could latch on to a part-time job through the trade journals.

The Confessions and Others

In recent years the confession magazines have been upgraded. In your mother's day these magazines were hidden from youngsters. Although some of them still lean toward the sensational, many are now slanted either toward the homemaker, or toward teenagers and their problems. A look at some of them will show you pages filled with recipes, articles on sewing, self-help material and homemaking hints, as well as fictional stories. In the past year, confession magazines carried articles on the following: children and integration; the magic teen years (describes the bodily changes taking place at this time); the story of why a supermarket manager gets ulcers; how a trained nurse can make money at a part-time nursing job; the story of a high-school marriage that tells why books and babies do not mix. Other subjects covered were: "How To Be Beautiful on Your Wedding Day," "The Handicapped Child," "How to Enjoy a Party," "Rules for Living with In-Laws."

What can *you* write about for the confession market? Every life is filled with stories, but not everyone is capable of writing his own story. Be a good listener. You might have to go no further than your own classroom for material. Maybe one of your classmates quit school to get married and she regrets her decision. Write an article from her angle, telling other young women why it is wiser to finish their education before taking on the responsibilities of married life.

Is one of your friends adopted? If he has opened up to you and has told you his problems, you can turn them into an article either from the viewpoint, "Be Glad You're Adopted," or "I Wish I Knew My Real Parents." You need not fear to use the facts he gives you, because you will change the names when you write. Confessions pay well and they pay promptly.

Many well-known writers started by selling stories to the confessions. The public is aware that the stories they once thought were true are actually written by skilled writers. Some readers send in personal experiences that staff writers put into acceptable form for publication. If you are unsuccessful in selling stories to the slicks, try some of the confession markets. The formula here is: sin, suffer, repent. Happiness or the promise of happiness must be held out to the reader at the end of the story. The male reader is likely to carry a lunch-box and the female is busy trying to stretch the budget. They want messages of hope; they want to think that tomorrow will be a better day. They buy magazines for inspiration. Reader-identification is important. Most of the stories are told from the viewpoint of a woman, but some men's stories are used, too. The *sin* in the story can be cruelty, jealousy, or misunderstanding in human relationships. The *problem* solved in the article must be one the reader can identify himself with; it should tell him how to be healthy, wealthy, or wise.

True Story is one of the magazines that uses surprise-ending short stories, paid for according to merit. Other stories sold there bring 5¢ per word, with possible bonus for outstanding writing. The magazine, at present, runs a "Women Are Wonderful" column that is thrown wide open to readers. Any contribution is used that backs up the theory that Women Are Wonderful: an original idea, an article, a cartoon, a bit of poetry. Payment is 5¢ for each published word; different rates apply for pictures and cartoons. Check a recent copy of the magazine for address.

Modern Romances holds annual contests and every story submitted to them is a contest entry. They award a new writer prize ($1,000) each year to a writer who makes his first sale to them that year. The editor, Henry P. Malmgreen, keeps in touch with writers by sending out a Newsletter. If you want to be on his mailing list to receive it and to get information about prize awards, send a postcard to him in care of the magazine, 750 Third Avenue, New York, 10017. There is no charge for this service.

When you study markets, you will see more than forty *women's magazines* listed and more than thirty devoted exclusively to male interests. Some of them are almost entirely staff-written. Many of them assign articles to professional writers. Your chances of selling to them are slim at first. Better stay with second-class markets until you are a top-flight writer! Be aware of these markets, however, and notice what they emphasize, just in case you want to try them occasionally. Women like to read about make-up, hair-styling, exercise, diet, fashions, food, budgeting, home maintenance, child rearing, self-improvement. Men are interested in adventure, automobiles, exposés, personality profiles, history, battle of the sexes, music, entertainment, dating, travel, military and medical information, hi-fi, sports, crimes and unusual criminals, mystery, disastrous events, adventures in exotic locales, treasure stories, and incidents from World War II, the Korean War, Viet Nam, and the Civil War.

The most encouraging marketing news in years for teenagers is the rash of new magazines known as 'teen publications. Some of them run contests or special columns for the work of young writers. (See Chapter VII.)

Chapter VI

IF IT COMES BACK

> *For no man can write anything who does not think that what he writes is, for the time, the history of the world.*
>
> —EMERSON

One of my students once asked me if I had ever sold an article after it had been rejected six times. My reply was, "I've sold an article after it has been turned down ten or fifteen times. I even have hopes for some of them after twenty rejections. Never give up trying to make a sale until you have exhausted every possible market! I rarely sell an article its first trip out."

Editors are just as eager to publish good material as you are to sell what you write. After all, they are in business to make money, and to achieve that end, they try to entertain their readers. They look forward to the mail with great anticipation, but most of the submissions go into the Slush pile instead of the *Rush* pile.

Some of the editors I have dealt with send a postcard the moment the manuscript arrives in their office, with the following information printed on it:

> Your manuscript, ___(Title)___, was received ___(Date)___. As soon as our editorial board has reached a decision, you will hear from us.

This practice puts the writer's mind at rest about whether or not his material was received. Unfortunately, not all editors do this and you may have to wait several months before you hear from them.

Editors sometimes apologize for holding a manuscript too long, as did this one at the *National Parent-Teacher* Magazine:

> I blush to think of how long we have kept your manuscript, "Passport to Understanding," without making any sort of report to you. We wanted—and still want—very much to use it, but we haven't yet been able to schedule it for a forthcoming issue.
>
> Would you mind our keeping the manuscript a little longer on a sort of tentative basis? You see, we accept very few unsolicited articles, and it's often difficult to find places for them among all the "must" material to which we are committed.
>
> If you wish us to return the manuscript in order that you may submit it elsewhere, we shall be happy to do so. Meanwhile many thanks for thinking of us and many apologies for our long silence.

I wrote back to the editor and told her to keep the manuscript as long as she wanted to, for I felt that she would eventually use the article. Some editors are not so considerate. They hold your manuscript for several months before giving you a reply. If you have not heard their decision within a month, you may write a follow-up letter. In most cases where I wrote to the editor to inquire about my manuscript, he sent the article back by return mail, and I wished that I had kept quiet.

Reasons for Rejection

When an article comes back, try to remember that there are many reasons why an editor cannot use it and that rejection does not necessarily imply lack of merit. Every month an editor receives more manuscripts than he can possibly use, even in the smaller publications. He might return yours because it is:

1. Unsuitable subject. Wrong slant.
2. Good subject, but does not make a point; fails to leave the reader better off than before reading it.

3. Lacking in research and facts.
4. In need of more *you* content.
5. A topic recently used.
6. Untimely material.
7. Too local or regional.
8. Without human interest.
9. Too long or too short.

Most printed rejection slips vaguely state, "Does not meet our present needs." The favorite form of address is, "Dear Contributor," but some of the cozier ones start, "Dear Friend." They come in all sizes on cards, sheets torn from memo pads, small and large stationery, and even in pamphlet form giving detailed requirements of the magazine. (You see, I have thrown away several shoe boxes full of them, and you will, too, before you start getting personal notes or checks.)

When an editor writes to you in long-hand, or when he sends you a personally signed typewritten note, your material is above average. A letter from him should encourage you to try other markets, and even to submit other manuscripts to him for consideration.

REWRITING

Editors of top slicks do not have time to work with you on revisions, but editors of second-class publications often make suggestions on how you can change your material to suit their needs. I have received notes from editors that have said:

"Cut to 350 words."
"Needs more case histories."
"We like this, but it's too fluffy for us. Can you do some more research?"
"Sorry we can't use this. Suggest you try *Today's Health.*"

One editor even wrote that my article sounded like *Reader's Digest* material! I am sorry to report that it drew only a complimentary letter from that editor instead of a check, but his words encouraged me to try another market, and I did sell the article to another magazine.

Whenever an editor takes time to suggest revisions, swallow your pride and get to work on them immediately. You may not agree with him, but he is your boss. When I submitted a 650-word article, "Quiet—Hospital Zone," to an editor, I thought it was as brief as I could make it. A note from him came in the next mail:

> Too long for our purposes. Would you consider trimming to 350 words? Please rewrite. Cut to 350 words.

I wondered how I could possibly throw away 300 of my precious words without ruining the message in the article. I thought it would lose its punch if I cut it, but I set to work for two reasons. One was that if I complied with the editor's request and returned a shortened manuscript to him within a day or two, he would feel that he could count upon me in the future to provide him with the type of article he wanted. (I was right. So far, he has bought over thirty articles from me.) The other reason was that the editor knew more about his space requirements and what his readers liked than I did. We are not always the best judge of our own work, and I felt that his opinion was more valuable than mine in this instance. Seeing the article in its shortened form, I had to admit that nothing was lost by cutting.

In your fervor to include all details in a manuscript, you sometimes put in some that are dull and that could be eliminated without changing the meaning of the whole. When you are forced to rewrite, those unnecessary sentences usually hit your eye without anyone telling you about them. You automatically cut out hackneyed expressions, cliches, bromides. Many times *a, an, the, but, and* can be dropped.

The several hours I spent on revising my article brought only a small check, but the lessons I learned were invaluable. Every article you rewrite will prepare you to write future articles with a greater economy of words.

Did you ever have a friend start to tell you a funny story, become sidetracked on an incident, and then end up blankly, "I've forgotten the funny part?" In writing, too, we often forget the "funny part," the punch line, the main point we are trying to communicate, because we digress with thoughts that do not pertain to the subject. You might not realize that you are including worthless information when you write your article the first time, but you will catch its irrelevance in your revision.

Only by rewriting can we sense whether or not we have used our material to its best advantage. We must dramatically present facts. Our sentences must have rhythm, not a monotonous beat. Finally, the article must be what experts refer to as "tight." All unnecessary material must be eliminated.

Someone has said that plucking harp strings *often* is not as important as knowing when to release them. The successful harpist must know when *to let go,* just as the understanding mother must let go the ties that bind her child to her, when he is old enough to make his own decisions. In article writing you have to know when to let go of material that is of no use to you. Perhaps you have a blind spot regarding your writing. You may want to read it to a friend, your teacher, or your parents. Perhaps they will see it from an angle that escapes you, and a few changes here and there could result in a sale instead of another rejection.

My only superstition about writing, though, is that I let no one see my work until it is in print. (No one close to me, that is. Only editors or their readers in editorial offices.) My reason is that criticism is often more *de*structive than *con*structive. If you discuss your writing with others, they say, "Well, now, here's the way I'd do it." Or, "Are you sure that's what you want to say? I'd write it this way." Or, "That's good, but I think this would be better." What you end up with is not an expression of your thoughts at all, but a hodge-podge of someone else's meandering ideas that completely blur your theme. Too much discussion about your work can easily kill its sparkle. I seldom talk about my writing. If I succeed, the world will know it soon enough; if I fail, only I know what happens to the unwanted manuscripts.

Points to Check

Re-read your article when it comes back from an editor. Check it for:

1. *Accuracy*. Do you have your facts straight? Are there any grammatical errors? Is the punctuation correct? Are there typographical errors?
2. *Coherence.* Have you put your point across? Do the sentences and paragraphs logically follow each other? Can the average reader understand what you are trying to say?
3. *Human interest.* Would the article catch your eye if you were thumbing through a magazine? Does it have emotional appeal? Is its theme a universal one?
4. *Structure.* Does it have a beginning, a middle, and an end? Could a person easily outline the main points? Does it:
   (a) Tell the reader what it is about in the first paragraph?
   (b) Follow through this main idea with specific points?
   (c) "Go out where it went in." Does the ending tie in with the beginning?

If you can find no flaws, if you still believe in the worth of your article, send it off *the same day* to another editor. If you feel, however, that it is not just right, or if an editor has asked you to rewrite it, start hacking it to pieces immediately. It is a painful process to throw away some of your paragraphs and to rearrange what is left into a meaningful pattern, but your reward could be a check.

Believe in Yourself

Do not let gloom weigh you down on those inevitable days when your manuscript turns up in your mailbox instead of money. Naturally you are discouraged because writing is a very personal sharing of yourself on paper. Even a factual trade-journal report has some of your knowledge and experience behind it; the article is colored with your personality. Every author reveals part of himself when he writes. When an editor says that he does not want to publish your manuscript, you feel that he has handed you a personal rebuff. No one except another writer can understand your secret hurt.

You have worked hard on your article. It represents many hours of real labor. Sometimes it comes back wrinkled or folded crookedly, and that means a retyping job. The paper-clip you so lovingly attached to the papers is missing. (I have lost hundreds of paper-clips that way.) Occasionally it is returned with coffee spilled on the pages. (Yes, that happened to two of mine. At least I know they were read!) If you are lucky, you will have to retype only the cover page; frequently the date the manuscript was received is stamped there in indelible ink, or the reader's initials are scrawled in the corner of the page, scratched so deeply that they cannot be erased. Console yourself with the thought that your work has not gone completely unnoticed.

Worst of all, you wonder if you will *ever* be a writer. How do you know whether or not your articles are good? Maybe you are just kidding yourself about your ability to write. In desperation, you seek out other writers. You turn to writers' clubs, classes on writing, or a mail-order course. Any of these could be beneficial IF the critic is well qualified to judge your work and *if* you are willing to take criticism. Too many times these aids to writing turn out to be a substitute for writing itself. If you are truly destined to be a writer, you work best alone, persistently, patiently, with quiet dedication.

After my minister's book had been turned down for the third time, he was in despair. "I don't know whether I can write or not," he confessed. "Putting words on paper is different from uttering them aloud in a sermon. I have to find out if I'm a writer or not before I can go on to writing anything else. What can I do?"

"Send it out again," I said. "Try another publisher." And then, remembering the topic he had spoken on the previous Sunday, I said, "You have to have faith!" Fortunately he has a sense of humor. He went back to his study, rewrote a section of his book, released his fears in prayer, and submitted the book, on faith, to another editor. He sold it. Today, having just finished his fourth book, he realizes the importance of believing in one's own ability.

The average person gives up at the first rejection slip. The above-average writer does not allow his spirit to be broken by one man's opinion, or by the criticism of several persons. Fannie Hurst weathered thirty-six rejections from the *Saturday Evening Post* before she sold them a story. In his book, *Think and Grow Rich,* Napoleon Hill says that to succeed in any line, you must be persistent. You need a *definite plan* and *a burning desire to achieve wealth* to reach that goal; in writing, too, you must have these qualities—a definite plan and a burning desire—to be a success, even in a small way.

Auntie Mame, which earned more than a million dollars in stage and screen rights and sold almost 300,000 hard-cover copies, was turned down by *fifteen* publishers before it finally appeared in print.

Whenever someone says with envy, "So you're a writer!" I try to appear humble. Whenever I get a rejection slip, I am humble without trying. In either case, I like to think of what Buddha said back in the 5th Century B.C.:

> As a solid rock is not shaken
> by a strong gale,
> so wise persons
> remain unaffected
> by praise or censure.

Chapter VII

OTHER FIELDS TO TRY

Look, then, into thine heart and write!

—LONGFELLOW

If is the biggest little word in the vocabulary of an inspiring writer. *If* I had a better education . . . *If* I had more time . . . *If* I had money . . . *If* I could travel . . . Do not let if-itis keep you away from your typewriter. You can write now, where you are, whatever your circumstances.

Not everyone enjoys writing articles. Your talents could lie in one of six other fields, but your job as a free-lance writer in any of them follows the same rules: study what is published, write something every day, and submit your work to editors.

SHORT STORIES

In its modern form, the short story was born and developed in America. Before its birth, there had been tales, stories, and narratives, but it was in reviewing Hawthorne's *Twice-Told Tales* that Poe set down what a short story should be. You cannot miss having a salable story today if you abide by the three points he emphasized:

(1) A short story should be short enough to be read at one sitting.
(2) The author should first decide upon the *single effect* he wishes to produce, and then invent characters, incidents, and situations to accomplish his intention.
(3) The structure of the story should be so economical that not a line could be left out without weakening the power of the story.

From Poe's time until now writers have been influenced by, and have tried to imitate O. Henry's snap endings, Sherwood Anderson's representationalism substituting for structure (importance of material or message over artistic effect), and the curt, masculine style of Hemingway.

The reason that no more good short stories are published than there are is that writers tend to write *incidents,* not complete stories. If you hope to write fiction, read the stories of famous writers. A good pocket edition is *50 Great Short Stories.* Study several books on the technique of writing fiction. Then, and only then, start to write your story.

Entering short story contests is one of the best ways to develop your short story writing skill because they give you a deadline to work toward, a check or some other prize if you win, and an opportunity (even if you lose) to find out how your work compares with other writers. At least four contests are run every year:

Writer's Digest annual short-short story contest open to all writers. Rules are usually published in the January issue of the magazine and winners are announced the following April. Prizes total $4,500.

Seventeen, 320 Park Avenue, New York, 10022, sponsors a short story contest each year for young people between the ages of thirteen and nineteen. Rules for the contest are carried in the March issue of the magazine. Prizes amounting to $1,000 (first prize, $500; second, $300; third, $100 and ten honorable mentions of $10 each) are given for short stories from 2,000 to 3,500 words.

Seventeen also pays for and publishes contributions by teenagers the year round. The editors say they are interested in seeing short stories, articles, or essays for the "You the Reader" department if:

1. You tell them your exact birthdate. (You must be between thirteen and nineteen.)

2. Your manuscript is typed.
3. You enclose a stamped, self-addressed envelope.

Your subject can be of any length and about anything you feel would be of interest to their readers.

Story, The Magazine of Discovery, started a new contest in 1966 with prizes of more than $6,500 for entries by college students in the following categories: short fiction, poetry, drama, biography, the essay (formal, critical, or light-informal), journalism (editorials, reporting, features), motion pictures, television, photo-essay, and the cartoon. Since the important creative work of tomorrow may come from college students, *Story's* contest is designed to encourage and bring early recognition to different kinds of talent emerging on campus. For copies of rules, send a postcard to The Director, *Story* Creative Awards, 53 W. 43 Street, New York, New York 10036. Winners of the April 15, deadline contest will be announced in the Fall issue of *Story*.

The *Scholastic Magazines* Writing Awards, designed to encourage creative writing among young people, are offered to students in public, private, and parochial schools across the country. Pupils in grades 10, 11 and 12 have six classifications open to them: short story, short-short story, poetry, informal article, formal article, and dramatic script. Students in grades 7, 8, and 9 may enter an article, poetry, or a short story. All entries must be submitted by their teachers, prepared in accordance with current rules, and accompanied by official entry blanks. They are carefully read by the editors of *Scholastic Magazines,* Inc., and top winners are selected by panels of nationally-known authors and educators. Awards include cash prizes, certificates of merit, and scholarships.

The national closing date for entries is the first of March. Regional closing dates are earlier. Rules booklets and entry blanks are available on request to *Scholastic Magazines* Writing Awards, 50 West 44th Street, New York, New York, 10036.

Guideposts magazine offers scholarship prizes in the sum of

$5,000 to high-school juniors and seniors, who may win a scholarship to the college of their choice by entering the annual contest. Here are the rules for the 1966 contest:

HIGH SCHOOL JUNIORS AND SENIORS
YOU MAY WIN A SCHOLARSHIP TO THE
COLLEGE OF YOUR CHOICE BY ENTERING

GUIDEPOSTS
3RD ANNUAL
WRITING CONTEST

For the third year in a row, *Guideposts* is sponsoring a writing contest for high school juniors and seniors. And it's an opportunity which is too good to miss. That's because this year's contest is bigger than ever—the scholarship prizes have been doubled from $2,500 to $5,000. To enter, this is all you need to do: tell us in 1,200 words or less about the person who has most helped you become stronger in your faith. The official theme is *How One Special Person Helped My Faith to Grow.* Manuscripts, which should be typed and double-spaced, must be postmarked by midnight, November 30, 1966, to be considered for one of the 10 scholarships which will be awarded in the following denominations: first prize, $2,000; second prize, $1,000; third prize, $750; fourth prize, $500; fifth prize, $250; sixth through tenth prizes, $100 each. The top article will be published in the April, 1967, issue of *Guideposts* along with a complete list of prize winners. Manuscripts will be judged by the editors of the magazine on the basis of sincerity, originality and story value.

THE OFFICIAL RULES:

1. The contest is open to all high school juniors and seniors attending school in the United States or U.S. possessions.

2. Manuscripts on the subject *How One Special Person Helped My Faith to Grow* must be typed, double-spaced, with a maximum of 1,200 words. Manuscripts should not deal with imaginary situations but must be the true personal experience of the writer.

3. All manuscripts must be the original work of the student submitting the entry.

4. All manuscripts must be mailed to Youth Contest, *Guideposts,* 3 West 29th Street, New York, New York 10001. Entries must be postmarked by midnight, November 30, 1966, and must include return address, plus

the name of the student's school. Winners will be notified by mail prior to the official announcement in the magazine.

5. All manuscripts become the property of *Guideposts* Magazine, Guidepost Associates, Inc., and cannot be returned.

6. Authors of the top 10 manuscripts, as judged by the editors of *Guideposts,* will receive scholarships to the accredited college or school of their choice:

First Prize:	$2,000
Second Prize:	$1,000
Third Prize:	$ 750
Fourth Prize:	$ 500
Fifth Prize:	$ 250
Sixth through Tenth Prizes:	$ 100 each

Scholarship awards will be administered by a committee named by *Guideposts.*

7. Prizes are not redeemable in cash and are not transferrable. All decisions of the judges are final.

8. Children of *Guideposts* employees and staff members are not eligible.

Additional copies of the official contest rules are available by writing *Guideposts,* 3 West 29th Street, New York, N. Y. 10001.

Watch writers' magazines for announcements of contests. *Writer's Digest* sponsors one annually just for article writers.

When you consider submitting manuscripts directly to the more than 100 short-short story markets, do not overlook the *little* or *literary* magazines. The pay is small; sometimes payment is in copies only, but the prestige value of having your work appear in them is immeasurable. Many of the literary magazines are connected with universities. If you cannot find them in your local library, you can get a copy by sending the price of one issue to the editor.

Teenage magazines especially welcome the work of young writers. Submissions for "Your Lively Arts" column in *Ingenue* average 1,000 a month. Manuscripts come from all over the United States, including Hawaii and Alaska, and from Canada, Hong Kong, Australia and other countries. Susan Thaler, editor of this section of the magazine, says that teenagers are sadly underestimated. They possess talent, sensitivity, conscience, humor, philosophical insight, courage, and intense religious belief.

Fiction selected for publication receives $25; poetry selected for publication receives $5; art work receives $25; bonus—one year's subscription to *Ingenue*.

Poetry

Most poets start writing at a very early age, possibly because to them, as Julian Dana said about the Very Young in *Lost Springtime,* "There is a freshness on the world, and every face and place and experience and idea and dream met for the first time is intriguing and demanding."

The first female poet in America, Anne Dudley Bradstreet, was married at sixteen. When she was eighteen years old, she came to New England with her father and her husband, both of whom became Governors of the Massachusetts Bay Colony. Anne despised the frontier environment and to sublimate her misery, she turned to writing poetry. Her brother-in-law was so impressed with her poems that he took them to London, where they were published in 1650.

William Cullen Bryant had an early start, too. At thirteen, he wrote an anti-Jefferson satiric poem. It was printed two years later. At seventeen, he wrote "Thanatopsis" and "To a Waterfowl," the most amazing achievements for a poet of that age in literary history. Six years later his father presented them to the *North American Review* without his knowledge and Richard Henry Dana suspected a hoax, because the quality of the style far exceeded that of even recognized American poets. When they were published, Bryant's reputation as a poet was established.

Robert Frost sold his first poem when he was fourteen. He worked as a bobbin boy in a mill, a Latin teacher in his mother's school, and as the editor of a weekly paper. While he was teaching, editing, and trying to be a shoemaker, he continued to write poetry—which editors refused. Some of them asked him not to submit any more and it was only after he moved to England, where two of his books were published, that he became famous.

He, who had left Harvard after two years' study, received more honorary degrees than any president.

After you have studied great poets and have read several textbooks on how to write poetry, there is nothing left for you to do but to *write*. Beginners often have their first literary attempts published in local newspapers. Sometimes the pay is only $1.00 per poem, but rewards other than cash are important. Publication in your hometown newspaper boosts your morale and increases your parents' and friends' esteem of you. The publicity you gain helps to establish you as a writer, for the more your name appears in print, the more often people will associate you with writing. If your poetry is published, clip it and paste it in a scrapbook. Someday when you apply for a job you can show it to a prospective employer. Or maybe you will read it to your grandchildren. The best satisfaction of all is seeing your own unique arrangement of words in type; only then do you know for sure that you are a writer.

Chester Kerr, Director, Yale University Press, gives this advice to fledgling poets, based on his experience with entrants for the Yale Series of Younger Poets competition:

First the *do's:*

Do enter such competitions as ours, and keep on entering them. The first try may not make it, but the subsequent ones just might. *Follow the rules to the letter.*

Do read authors' periodicals such as *The Writer,* which announce poetry competitions.

Do stick to the shorter and simpler forms, such as the sonnet and the villanelle, until you become more experienced.

Do keep writing, and writing, *and* writing.

Second, the *don'ts:*

Don't send rambling personal letters with your manuscript; they only antagonize the editor.

Don't submit long narrative poems for a competition unless they specify such works.

Don't try experiments until you've mastered the accepted forms; they're hard enough.

Don't bother with lurid writing or "shock" words; we've seen them all before.

Don't ask for a criticism with a submission unless you are submitting to a department whose purpose is critical.

Broadly speaking, one can only advise young poets to write all they can, to submit constantly, both to competitions and to periodicals, and to send in clean, double-spaced typed manuscripts.

For book collections of poetry, university presses are probably the best bet for new writers. Take a look at their catalogues, and write to any and all who publish contemporary verse.

There are hundreds of markets for good poetry, ranging from top-circulation slicks to small publications devoted entirely to verse. Big magazines pay high rates; the smaller ones pay very little, perhaps a token fee, book awards, or contributors' copies only. Many of the little magazines, however, are highly respected and they give the poet an audience that understands and appreciates poetry.

In submitting poetry, use the standard 8½x11 typing paper. Your name and address should appear on each page. Send only a few poems to one magazine at a time and enclose a stamped, self-addressed envelope for their return in case the editor finds them unusable. When you are considering where to sell your poetry, remember that markets are divided into four categories:

(1) General magazines
(2) Literary and "little" magazines
(3) Verse magazines
(4) Greeting-card verse publishers

Religious and denominational magazines use poetry, as well as juvenile magazines, and that is why you should subscribe to a writer's magazine, so that you can be in touch with what is going on in the publishing world at the moment. Requirements change rapidly. One of the changes reported in the March, 1963, issue of *The Writer* concerns greeting cards. Carl Goeller, research director for Rust Craft Greeting Cards, reported:

> A brand-new addition to the "juvenile" field is the *teen-age* card. This is the newest thing in the greeting card field, and so far is the least explored. Editors frankly admit this market is so new they have very few touchstones by which to judge ideas, but they will hasten to add that they are hungry for good fresh approaches to teen cards, and that they'll pay well for them.
>
> There are two kinds of teen-age cards—those which are to be sent by adults to a teen-ager, and those which are sent to teen-agers by teen-agers. A further sub-division is often recognized—that of age. Publishers make cards for teen-agers in the thirteen-to-fifteen-year-old bracket, who seem to prefer the lighter, clever card, and for the sixteen-to-nineteen-year-olds, who lean toward the humorous and studio type.
>
> Publishers *have* discovered one important fact about teen-age cards. Those which attempt to appeal to the teen-ager by "talking his language" with the latest slang have been extremely unsuccessful. Either the adults writing the cards are just "not with it" or the slang used is not universal throughout "teendom." Keep your teen-age cards breezy but very generally sendable, add a touch of novelty, and you can sell the teen-age card editor.
>
> These, then, are the major changes in this changing industry. The writer who is aware of them is miles ahead. The writer who takes advantage of them stands to crack the market wide open.

You are fortunate if you live in a community where a writing class can give you help with your poetry, honest criticism, evaluation, and suggestions for marketing it. If you have no help, you may want to submit your poems to The Poet's Workshop, published in *The Writer*. Rules for submitting poems to the column are as follows:

1. Poems must be original, submitted by the author, unpublished, and not under consideration by another publisher.
2. Poems should be typewritten on standard typing paper, and the name and address should appear on each page.
3. There should be only one poem on a page.

4. Poems should not be longer than about 20 lines.

5. No manuscripts will be acknowledged or returned. Unfortunately the volume of submissions makes it impossible for us to enter into any correspondence in connection with this column.

6. Keep carbon copies of your poems, for all poems are destroyed after the selection of the month has been made.

7. Poets may submit as many poems as they wish at any time. Poems that arrive too late for consideration in a particular column are held over for the next.

8. No payment is made for the poems published in this column.

9. Send poems to "The Poet's Workshop," *The Writer,* 8 Arlington St., Boston, Mass. 02116.

FILLERS

Goethe once wrote, "The smallest hair throws its shadow." Maybe your influence as an author will start in a small way by writing fillers that throw a hair-like line of knowledge in a thousand directions.

Fillers range from a few lines up to 500 words and some editors pay as much as $100 or $150 for them. They cover jokes, anecdotes, epigrams, puzzles, curious facts, satires, inspirational incidents, and how-to items. Over seventy magazines use filler material. If your writing time is limited and if you have a knack for short, pithy sayings, you could earn a fairly regular income from writing fillers.

Watch for filler material when you read magazines, and then submit any appropriate items you have. Also look for contests seeking jokes, solutions to personal problems, letters, etc. You will notice that some short material, such as recipes, is staff-written. On the other hand, many magazines run monthly columns using special type fillers. *Reader's Digest* pays $100 for "Life in These United States" column and $100 for "Humor in Uniform." Contributions are not acknowledged or returned, but items not accepted within ninety days may be considered rejected. The author is then free to send the material elsewhere. The magazine also uses items for "Picturesque Speech" and "Patter."

Everywoman's Family Circle has a column where readers share experiences on bringing up children. Each solution to a child-rearing problem brings $10. You need not be a parent to submit to this column. Perhaps you could report an experience your mother had with you or with your brothers or sisters, or something that happened in the home of a neighbor or a friend. *True Experience* pays $5 for "Out of the Mouths of Babes" anecdotes; letters on "The Most Interesting Person I Have Ever Known" bring $10; 250-word letters on any subject printed under the heading, "What Do You Think?" bring $10. *Together* magazine uses church-related stories, as do several of the religious magazines. Many publications want tips on home-making, short cuts to housekeeping, and suggestions for unusual decorating ideas.

Since requirements change with new columns being added and old ones dropped, study recent issues of magazines before sending in your fillers. Keep a file folder up-to-date both with published fillers and with material that you are working on. Use the same form in typing your fillers as you do for other manuscripts. Type only one filler to a page. Short jokes can be typed on 3x5 cards. Enclose a stamped, self-addressed envelope unless the magazine specifies that no material will be returned.

PLAYS

When you think about plays, what words come to your mind? Names of famous playwrights, producers, directors, backers or "angels," critics. Most of all, though, you see Broadway, the famous White Way, where you would like for the name of your play to be up in lights. The idea is not as far-fetched as you might suppose. You do not need to take a jet to New York. Your only requirements are a jet-propelled imagination, proper equipment for the writing journey, and grim determination to stick with it, no matter how many air pockets or forced landings you encounter. You can write plays in your own hometown, in your house, in your room.

Experts advise that you submit your script to a little theatre group in your part of the country. If you know about an amateur theatre or a college theatre in your area, write to the director and ask if he uses original plays. (For more information on who is looking for plays, check the May, 1962, issue of *The Writer,* 8 Arlington St., Boston, Mass. You can probably find a copy in your local library.)

Each year there are several playwriting contests, most of them sponsored by universities, that pay the winners up to 1,000 dollars. Tennessee Williams started his career by winning a contest sponsored by the Theatre Guild of Webster Groves, Missouri.

Television Scripts

How many times have you seen a television show when you have said, "I could write a better script than that!"? Maybe you were annoyed by a trick ending that appeared to be tacked on with no relation to the rest of the script, poor characterization, or a lagging plot. If you like to write suspense—the type of script where the hero is faced with apparently unsurmountable odds, and then manages to extricate himself from the hopeless situation in the nick of time—you may want to try writing for TV.

There are so many stories on television today that we are inclined to think that this is an easy field to break into; however, it is most difficult and only a handful of submitted scripts qualify. Before you start to write, study samples in library books. Visit a local television station. It is a good idea to contact the manager ahead of time. He will give you permission to see what goes on behind the scenes in a live telecast and he will give you discarded paper work, so that you can study the format. For example, here is a sample page of the TV script of *Star-Trek,* a science fiction opus:

STAR TREK

"The City on the Edge of Forever"
written by Harlan Ellison

FADE IN:
ESTABLISHING SHOT—ANGLE IN SPACE

The USS ENTERPRISE hanging in mid-f.g. over a strange, silvery planet under a wan and dying red sun. CAMERA MOVES IN on ship and OVER this (and subsequent pantomime shots), we HEAR the VOICE of KIRK:

KIRK'S VOICE (OVER)

Ship's Log: star-date 3134.6. Our chronometers still run backward. We have followed the radiations to their planet-source here at the Rim of the Galaxy, but something else is happening . . .

(beat)

When we left Earth each of the 450 crew-members of the Enterprise was checked out stable. But it's been two years—so much stress on them. We have continuous psych-probes, but we know some have been altered. Even some who may have gone sour: we can't know till the flaw shows up. And by then, it's too late . . . much too late . . .

While VOICE OVER carries, CAMERA MOVES IN on Enterprise smoothly till we

RAPID LAP-DISSOLVE TO:

INT. ENTERPRISE—BECKWITH'S CABIN—EXT. CLOSEUP

on a small, isometrically-shaped metal container as it is opened by a hand. VOICE OVER is heard (after beat) as we HOLD CLOSE on the lid of the box, opening with tambour doors, so the interior of the box rises and a strange DULL LIGHT FLOODS the FRAME. As the container opens, the black velvet interior slides up to reveal possibly half a dozen glowing jewels. They are faceted solids, but not stone; more like a hardened jelly that burns pulsing with an inner light: gold, blue, crimson. As KIRK'S VOICE OVER ends we hear:

LeBEQUE'S VOICE O.S.

(trembling)

Beckwith, stop it! Give me one!

CAMERA PULLS BACK to MED. 2-SHOT showing LT/JG LeBEQUE, a French-Canadian with a strong face—a face now beaded with sweat, a face in torment—and another officer, . . .*

In this type of writing you have little chance to open doors if you submit material cold; it is best to work through an agent. Some of them charge initial reading fees. Others do not. Instead of sending a completed manuscript, query the agent first about his terms. You can find a list of agents who handle television scripts and their addresses in the May, 1961, issue of *Author & Journalist* magazine.

Novels

The fact that you are a new, unpublished writer has nothing to do with your success or failure in writing the great American novel, every true author's secret ambition. If you have something to say, and if you say it well, you have just as much opportunity as anyone else to see your book published. Doubleday & Co., Inc., reported that in 1960 they published 91 novels, 21 of which were *first* novels. In 1961 they published 95 novels, 29 of which were *firsts.* That is only one publishing house of almost 300 book publishers. Every manuscript submitted received sympathetic attention, because the editors want to please the public and to make money, and to discover a new talent adds stature to their organization.

It is a rare writer who hits the target the first time. Many writers have several unpublished novels in a trunk before they finally see one in print. Do not be discouraged if your book is turned down by the first editor who sees it. Submit it to another one. Some authors send only an outline and three sample chapters; if the editor is interested, he asks to see the remainder of the book. You can find editors' requirements in your market lists.

Once you have tried to write a novel, your respect for published writers knows no bounds. Never again will you read for

* Reprinted courtesy Harlan Ellison and Star-Trek, NBC, and *Writer's Market,* 1967.

sheer pleasure. You will continually ask yourself, "Why did this author succeed when I failed?" And if you study enough, write enough, and work hard enough, some day you will see *your* book on a best-seller list.

Chapter VIII

HAZARDS OF FREE-LANCING

> *It is evident that no professional writer can afford to write only when he feels like it. If he waits till he is in the mood, till he has the inspiration as he says, he waits indefinitely and ends by producing little or nothing.*
>
> —W. Somerset Maugham

A free-lance writer's relation to his editors is a strange one. They rarely meet face to face. While some free-lancers visit editorial offices and work directly with editors on assignments, the average writer who works on a part-time basis sits at his typewriter in a cubicle in one city and tries to reach the mind of a man behind a desk in another city. Whether or not he is successful in convincing that mind that what he has to offer is worthy of publication is an unbelievable combination of luck, correct slanting, intelligent marketing, and timing. If he can find two or three editors who like his work, he should try to continue to supply what they want, for his chances of making sales are much better than if he just casts his bait hit or miss in the vast publishing sea.

Writers feel that the editors sometimes give them a hard row to follow and editors often think that these dreamers are difficult persons to deal with, yet each depends upon the other for an income.

The 1950 census showed that there were 15,000 professional authors in the nation. No one knows exactly how many part-time writers there are, for some quit every day and a few new ones sit down at their typewriters. As with every business, there are certain hazards peculiar to the occupation. It may help you to know that other writers face the same problems you do—and conquer them.

Your Time Is Your Own

If someone told you that he could go to work when he wanted to, watch the clock as often as he wished, take as much time off for lunch as he pleased, and leave work at any time of day, you would think he had a soft job, would you not? As a writer, you can manage your working hours any way you please, but that very freedom is the biggest hazard writers have. It is easy to say that you will set aside a certain time each day or each week for writing and let nothing interfere with it, but no one outside the profession understands your need for rigid hours and they unwittingly intrude on your privacy with telephone calls requesting that you give book reviews, take over the chairmanship of a publicity committee at school, or write news items gratis for your community paper. Everyone loves a writer. Somehow you are considered to be above average in education. "With your talent, we need you," is the plea. Once the word gets around that you are a writer, you have to learn to say "No" to the demands on your time. I know a girl who was writing a book against great odds; she was part of a big family that was forever celebrating birthdays, anniversaries, and holidays. She had a deadline to meet at the publisher's, and to avoid hurting anyone's feelings, she rented a room in a downtown hotel until her book was finished.

The only way you can become a selling writer is to devote all of your spare time to writing and to reading. Minutes are precious to you now more than ever, if you are carrying a heavy work load at school. But even while you are busy with other tasks, you must think as a writer, read as a writer, act as a writer. You spend a great many hours alone; of course, you take some time off to mingle with others, but social engagements should not be used as excuses for not writing.

When he is alone, every writer invents his own little excuses to keep him from getting down to work. He wants to write, but part of him procrastinates. He sharpens pencils, looks through old file folders, cleans his typewriter. One way to force yourself to start typing is to put a sheet of paper in the typewriter at the end of one day's stint and leave a half-finished sentence on it so that you will have to look at it the next day.

You have to battle with yourself constantly to make intelligent use of your time. There are days, no matter how hard you try, when you cannot write at all. This is known as writer's slump.

Writer's Slump

The writer's slump periodically hits professionals as well as beginners. No shot is available to ward it off; it strikes without warning and you must suffer through the illness, just as you do the common cold. You sit at the typewriter and stare at an empty page. No checks come in the mail to renew your faith in yourself. Maybe several rejection slips plunge you further into despair. Those printed impersonal slips of paper underline your secret feeling about yourself: "I'm not a writer. I'm a failure."

Some literary authorities insist that there is no such thing as a mental block for a writer. You simply reach a plateau. Whatever you name this *thing,* it creeps up on you and leaves you as helpless as if your hands were tied behind you. Your non-productive period is agony. You long to create. You produce nothing. After you have lived through several of these valleys of the shadow, you become more philosophical about each succeeding one because you know they are only temporary.

Mary Roberts Rinehart wrote:

It is a curious thing, this matter of creative writing. There are times when the well apparently goes entirely dry. For fourteen months, five years ago, I was as arid as the Sahara. Another time such a period lasted almost a year. I believe it is common to all writers, and, so far as I know, there is nothing to do but wait until the well fills up again. It does, almost invariably. But attempting to work at such times is like pushing against a closed door. It only closes it tighter.

Then some morning it is over. The creative mind—whatever it may be—commences to function again. The well is full; perhaps it always has been full. The sense of failure passes. The sun shines . . .

I have found that any one of eight mechanical aids, and sometimes a combination of all of them, can start me writing again. Try them and see which ones work best for you.

When you just do not know what to write about, you can:

1. *Buy a writer's magazine.* Look on the newsstands for one you do not subscribe to and devour everything in it, including the ads. I write to several magazines I find in market lists that offer free copies of their publication. I mail requests for free writers' tips to every magazine that advertises them.

2. *Query an editor about an article.* Although I do not ordinarily work from a query, I find that there is nothing like a deadline to make one get to work. I once wrote to an editor and asked if he would be interested in an article on the problems of the "only" child. A "Yes" answer forced me to change my notes around and to expand them into a completed manuscript, whereas if I had not had a market in sight, I would have dropped the idea.

3. *Rework old material.* When new thoughts elude you, spend two hours a day rewriting what is in your rejected file. I often force myself to put a blank sheet of paper in the typewriter and to start fresh on an old project. Even though my creative powers are at a low ebb, the actual process of typing brings up ideas from my subconscious.

4. *Call two friends you have not talked to for a long time.* Article writers especially profit from chance remarks that can be turned into cash. As a rule, I consider long phone conversations a waste of time, but when I cannot write, I catch up on my visit-

ing and replenish my empty spirit at the same time. One of my friends remarked, "Women talk too much." That sounded like a good title. I jotted it down while I listened to her and I later sold an article based on those four words. Another friend said during a telephone conversation, "You know, I think you met your husband at just the right time in your life. A year or so earlier he would not have appealed to you." She started me to thinking about the importance of timing in our lives, another article that sold.

5. *Go to the library and hunt for two or three books about writers or writing.* Pick up biographies of famous writers. Study great literature of the past. Read technical how-to-do-it books. You gain inspiration from reading.

6. *Read magazines.* One day when I was reading advertisements in a magazine, I was struck by the catchy lines at the top of the ads that suggested article ideas. The words opened up several new areas of thought:

(a) "Merry Christmas in September!" (S & H Green Stamps)
(b) "People aren't pretzels—" (Chrysler Corp.)
(c) "Indulge Yourself . . ." (Sanka)
(d) "Should Your Child Be a Physicist?" (New York Life Insurance Co.)
(e) "Don't Be a Vidiot" (Kimble Glass Co.)

I would not use these as titles for articles, merely as points to take off on opinions of my own.

7. *Get excited about a cause, a group, a person, a goal, a rebuff, a compliment. Be alive.* Maybe you could not write anything significant lately because your life has been too placid, too routine. When writing is difficult perhaps you need to accept a social engagement or to attend a function that you would ordinarily turn down.

8. *Give your mind a rest.* The only way to find water in a desert is to hunt for an oasis. While you are waiting to discover that fertile spot in your brain, you can tread sand by cleaning

your typewriter, rearranging your files, cleaning your room. In my last burst of physical energy, I painted the basement stairway, all the doors inside and out, and a utility cabinet. Once I was able to hobble back to my desk, ideas came fast. Physical activity stimulates mental processes.

As long as you have established a deadline for yourself, the so-called "hopeless" days will not ruin your total output. Say to yourself on a Monday morning, "Next Monday I am going to mail an article." Even if you cannot write for two or three days, you will finish the article on time. Some writers keep on writing through the slump with the knowledge that they will eventually throw most of their papers away.

SOMEONE KILLS YOUR IDEA . . .

Often a good article does not sell because the editor kills its timeliness by holding it too long before making a decision on it, or the idea may be so timely that someone else beats you to it in print.

I once wrote an article about teaching foreign languages in grade school when that notion was first catching public interest. I had spent several hours in the public library doing research on the topic; I had consulted the *Reader's Guide to Periodical Literature* and had looked up the very few articles that had been published on the subject at that time. Then I made an appointment with a Romance Languages professor at the University of Cincinnati. After interviewing him, I worked on the article for several days before I mailed it to him for his O.K. Another typing was required before I could send the manuscript to an editor. She held the article for *eight* months, and when she finally decided to reject the manuscript due to an overloaded schedule, it was too out-of-date to submit anywhere else. (This was a rare case. Most editors accept or reject a manuscript within two or three months.) With some additional research, I could have rewritten it to include foreign language courses that had been added to school curricula throughout the land since the inception of the article, but upon further checking I discovered that several articles on the subject had been published in the interim. The idea was no longer fresh and new. Any more time I spent on it would have been wasted. I put the manuscript aside, apologized to the professor for taking up so much of his time, and went on to something else.

Another article I did on the subject of rebound tumbling went out to more than one editor before it was held for awhile. I had spent many hours in the library reading pamphlets on the topic; I had interviewed a man in my town who was in charge of operating one of the tumbling centers, and I had sent three letters to out-of-towners, two men in the business of constructing nets and a university coach who could tell me about national champions in this sport. All three contacts had replied immediately with facts and pictures. I thought I had an excellent subject for an article. I sent it out about eight months ahead of the time I hoped to see it in print, a Spring issue. By the time that two editors had held it for three months each, I had to change the slant when I sent it out again because it was too late for a summer edition. I finally abandoned the article because the last editor who rejected it wrote me that interest in the sport was waning, since there had been accidents in connection with it and only experts were completely safe in trying it. I returned the pictures to the men who had sent them to me and explained why the article did not sell.

It is disheartening to put a great deal of time and thought into a piece of writing for which you get nothing in return, but that is one of the risks you take in free-lancing. Editors are not to blame. They have problems, too.

One time I interviewed the manager of a large country store. He mentioned casually that a reporter from a national magazine had been there about a month before and had taken some pictures, but he did not know if the article would ever appear. I went ahead and wrote mine. The day I was going to drop it in the mail, a big spread on the same topic came out in a Sunday supplement; I dropped my work into the wastebasket. There was no use to try to sell it to a smaller magazine, because the editor would have thought that I had simply rehashed what had already been published.

Such examples can be multiplied by any free-lancer. After awhile you develop an optimistic attitude and comfort yourself with the thought that professionals say they are lucky if they sell 50 percent of what they write. So what are you worrying about?

What Happened to Your Ms.?

Launching a manuscript is comparable to watching a plane take off into the wild blue yonder. You do not know when it will reach its destination or whether or not it will come back. The other day I received an airmail letter from California. A manuscript that I had sent to a magazine three years before was being returned to me. Between the date when I had submitted the article and the date it was sent back, the editor had died and the magazine had evidently limped along through many changes in personnel. My follow-up letters had gone unanswered. I had filed my carbon in my *Idea* file, in the hope that some day I might rewrite the article and submit it to another magazine. Now I was free to rewrite it, but insofar as I was concerned, the idea was dead. My enthusiasm for the subject was gone. I no longer cared to work on it. I threw it away. I admit that this was an extreme case; most of the time you hear from an editor within a month.

I was more fortunate with the "Garden of Hope." I had originally slanted the article for an Easter issue of a religious magazine. Once again an editor held a manuscript too long. I rewrote the lead when I got it back and sent the article to several magazines. It always bounced back. I had to wait a year before I sent it out again with the Easter angle. Because of an error in my filing system that I did not notice until the manscript was in the mail, I sent it back to the same editor who had rejected it in the first place. What happened? You guessed it! He sent me a check. I suppose that one of four possibilities had occurred: a change in editors, or the one who worked there had a short memory, or he had a change of heart, or my article came in the second time when there was a shortage of manuscripts.

They Changed It!

Nothing hurts a writer more (except receiving rejection slips) than to have someone change his words without asking his permission. "They" are blamed for this. Who are "they?" No one is quite sure. I secretly think that frustrated writers on editorial staffs get boundless pleasure from using the blue pencil. Of course, no editor would allow your meaning to be completely changed. They often change or drop little words, pet phrases, titles, endings.

The first article I ever sold was about a hiking trip in the Smoky Mountains. The editor of a travel magazine embroidered almost every line. I nearly choked when I read that flowers were "blooming merrily along the trail." *That* I would never say! The title he chose—"Go Feet!"—was better than my prosaic, "Hiking in the Smokies." As I endorsed the $50 check that seemed very large to me then, I forgave him for his corrections.

Sometimes an editor sends you a proof sheet before your article is printed so that you can approve changes. The editor at *Together* magazine did this with one of my articles and I felt better about the changes than if he had made them without my permission.

Low Pay

When you keep track of the time you spend writing and an account of your income, you find that your hourly pay is low. Reading, gathering material, assembling it, typing it, mailing it, and the mental agony you endure all add up to small rewards. We read about fabulous earnings from television and movie rights. We tend to think of writers as privileged souls who live in untold splendor and wealth. Compared with a business tycoon at the top of his profession, the writer is underpaid. Besides, he might have one best seller in ten years. Rare is the man who turns out a money-maker every year or even every three or four years. He has to live on something in-between breaks. That is why so few people turn to writing full time.

You are probably the happiest kind of writer, because you do not depend upon writing for your bread and butter; what you earn from it is icing on the cake.

If free-lancing is so hazardous, why do I suggest that you try it? Because the rewards are greater than the drawbacks. H. L. Mencken once wrote to Will Durant:

> You ask me, in brief, what satisfaction I get out of life, and why I go on working. I go on working for the same reason that a hen goes on laying eggs. There is in every living creature an obscure but powerful impulse to active functioning. Life demands to be lived.*

A writer cannot deny life. He must record it as he sees it. He cannot help himself. With Mencken he feels, "Only the dying can be really idle."

* *Letters of H. L. Mencken,* edit. by Guy S. Forgue, Alfred A. Knopf, Inc., New York.

Chapter IX

THE REWARDS

> *I can shake off everything if I write; my sorrows disappear, my courage is reborn . . . I can recapture everything when I write, my thoughts, my ideals, and my fantasies . . .*
>
> —ANNE FRANK

A writer spends his working hours alone, but he is never lonely. The most prolific author is at a loss for words when he tries to explain this feeling to non-writers. As long as he is caught up in the excitement of creation, he is lifted beyond himself to the extent that nothing else matters to him at the moment; heat, cold, hunger, thirst cease to exist for him. Through writing he is transported to another world beyond his four walls.

But just as writing is an escape for him, it is also a means of bringing him closer to his fellow man.

INFLUENCE

Do you remember the story about little Virginia who wrote to the *New York Sun* to ask if there was a Santa Claus? She said that her father said if you saw a fact in the *Sun,* it was so. People today still tend to believe what they see on the printed page. Never underestimate the power of the press. The smallest newspaper item influences minds. As Rabelais once said, "The thing is written. It is true." You have no idea how many persons will read, and take to heart, what you have written. That is one reason why you must be absolutely accurate. If you make a mistake when you are speaking, you can take back your words and be forgiven on the spot, but if you err in print, retraction is more difficult.

Even unknown writers receive fan mail. I am always surprised that in this bustling world men and women take time from their busy schedules to write to me or to a magazine in which my work has appeared. A congratulatory letter concerning an article, "Your Job and You," came from an executive of a large company in Illinois. A girl in Brooklyn wrote to me one time for more information about a record I had mentioned in another article. A man in Missouri wrote to the editor of a magazine to ask how he could start a club similar to one I had written about.

Besides writing for an immediate audience, you pass something on in permanent form to future generations. The author of a book must be especially pleased at the thought that many years hence someone will take his book off a library shelf and read it. We think of periodicals as being transitory, but when your magazine articles are listed in the *Reader's Guide,* it is quite possible that students, teachers, and other readers will call for them out of the stacks for years to come.

Prestige

From the early days of picture-writing carved or painted on palaces, temples, and tombs, mankind has respected writers, the recorders of history. Without writers, no books would tell us of the past; no newspapers and magazines would give us information about happenings in all parts of the world. We have come a long way since man kept count of his possessions and marked the passage of time by making notches in sticks or knots in strings. The Incas of Peru kept their records by means of knotted cords. Today we take writing, as we know it, for granted, but no one ever takes the writer himself for granted. He is accorded a special pedestal in our society.

Why will friends and acquaintances look up to you if you write? Because they see you as an educated person (if not in book knowledge, at least in experience), as a disciplined person who makes good use of his time, and as a person of conviction who is not afraid to express his ideas. Doors that remain forever closed to others are opened to writers. Everyone knows the value of good publicity. Most persons are agreeable to being interviewed. Librarians help you in your research. Relatives stand in awe of a writer in the family. Outsiders think you are set apart from the common man.

I discovered this in a small way the other evening when a student called from the university to ask me for an alumni pledge. He was part of a telephone committee to collect funds, and after I had renewed my pledge, he said, "By the way, I see that you have a Certificate in Journalism. I'm thinking about switching over to that field. What's it like?" I tried to answer his question briefly. What amused me was the awe in his voice when I told him I was a free-lance writer working at home. To him I was one of the great voices of our time, the epitome of success, tops in achievement. As I hung up in a warm glow, I thought wryly that I could not spend what the boy had just given me, and yet the greatest rewards for the free-lancer are not measured in dollars and cents.

Meeting People

Leads for articles take you down pathways you might otherwise never explore. If you like to do the interview article, you will spend many interesting hours learning far more than you ever put into your manuscripts. One afternoon I interviewed another writer in her spacious living-room overlooking a Kentucky lake. Our conversation led us to her collection of cookbooks, and I came away with an increased interest in cooking. One woman showed me her collection of Delft ware; another had salt and pepper shakers in all sizes from every state in the Union. I talked to a woman who raises parakeets and to a doctor whose hobby is raising homing pigeons. One time I visited a leather company and another time an apple farm. Without exception, everyone I ever contacted with a view toward writing about his business or hobby replied with enthusiasm.

Your love for writing draws other writers to you. You also

make friends in allied fields. You may think that working at home takes you out of circulation, but you can be in touch with the publishing business through the mails. One young writer exchanges Christmas cards with an editor, even though they have never met. When he ordered a book from another writer, the author enclosed a letter wishing him success with his own work. Writers are a closely knit group. Free-lancers especially sympathize with each others' problems.

INNER SATISFACTION

Why are you a writer?

I asked that question to six writers. If I had asked 600, their answers would have followed the same line of thinking:

1. "I'm happy when I write."
2. "I can't help myself. I'm compelled to write."
3. "Something seems to be pushing me on."
4. "It's my way of letting off steam."
5. "I want to feel that I am of use to others."
6. "I'm miserable when I'm not writing."

Joseph Conrad wrote of the dark mood that attacks writers when their work is not going well. In a letter to a friend, Edward Garnett, who was a reader for a London publisher, he wrote:

> My dear Garnett
>
> I am not dead tho' only half alive. Very soon I shall send you some Ms. I am writing hopelessly—but still I am writing. How I feel I cannot express. Pages accumulate and the story stands still.
>
> I feel suicidal.
>
> . . .
>
> I am afraid there's something wrong with my thinking apparatus. I am utterly out of touch with my work—and I can't get in touch. All is darkness.*

* From *Letters from Joseph Conrad,* edited by Edward Garnett, copyright 1928 by The Bobbs-Merrill Company, Inc., R. 1956 by David Garnett, reprinted by permission of the publishers.

For every writer those moments of darkness come and he is at a loss to describe them. When he is writing again, he experiences an inner satisfaction that seems maudlin when he tries to put it into words. His challenge is in the creation of pages that capture thoughts, conversations, elusive fleeting moments. Many writers lose interest in their work once it is print. They never read it again. They refuse to see plays or movies of their scripts.

For me (and I hope for you) article writing is one way to give form and substance to the fragile feelings of daily living and to share them with others.

On the other hand, maybe writing short stories is your best method for self-expression. Here is a short story written by a 17-year-old girl, Michelle Lundborg, of Denver, Colorado. When it was published, the editor printed this paragraph at the end of the story: "If you wish to answer this plea, write to: Sixteenth Autumn, *Ingenue* Magazine, 750 Third Ave., New York 17, N. Y. Best letters will be published in a future issue." The story brought the greatest response the magazine had ever had from readers.

YOUR LIVELY ARTS
A sampling of the best of today's teen artists and writers

SIXTEENTH AUTUMN

Could your love stand up against the prejudice of your closest friends?

A SHORT STORY BY MICHELLE LUNDBORG, 17
Machebeuf H. S., Denver, Colo.

I can't adequately describe to you how beautiful this park is in late summer and early fall. May, June, and July—the months most people love—are fresh, sweet, lovely months here; but August, September, and October are practically indescribable. Their beauty lies in their richness, their crispness, their color. Unless you've seen this park in autumn, in its conflagration of deep, deep browns, reds, and burnt oranges; smelled its earthy smell; felt the scratch of its dry leaves; tasted its smoky flavor, heard its constant rustling whisper—a master poet couldn't completely recreate its beauty for you.

I'm telling you about the park and about fall because I couldn't do justice to the story of Rick without them. The three of them, the park, fall, and Rick, whole and complete within themselves, form a unity—a unity that cannot be broken without detracting from one of the wholes.

Listen . . . has something ever happened to you that seemed so important, so very important that you felt you had to share it to better understand what it means to you? Then you'll understand why I'm sitting here trying so hard to explain this to you. Trying to make you understand. Trying to justify myself, I guess.

And here we are in this park. But there are no more reds, browns, or oranges now. No more deepness, richness. Only starkness, bleakness. I don't really like winter. Its coldness and its detachment depress me; and on quiet, gray days like this one, it even frightens me. It's hard for me to believe that this white and black panorama of March was once the autumn scene I tried to describe to you before. So let's try to forget it's March. Forget about this cold, bare ground we're sitting on. Ignore your cold feet and your numb hands. Remember autumn, and maybe that will help you to understand.

I had come to the park that day because the weather was gorgeous and the park seemed to be the perfect place to finish the novel that was due for English class the next day. I wasn't too crazy about the book, I can remember, and I figured the park would offer the least chance of putting the book down in favor of something more interesting. Not so. After about fifty pages, I couldn't concentrate any more. I got up from this same tree we're sitting under now, only then it was red and brown and orange, and shuffled through the crunchy leaves to the duck pond. How I love that pond! Especially in autumn. Those tiny little waves just lap so gently against those rocks, and the moss is so green. There were maybe five ducks on the pond that day. They were all swimming together and making those queer noises you've heard ducks make. The brownish one kept nibbling at the speckled one's wing. The more the one nibbled, the louder the other one quacked. I started laughing. I think if you could have seen them you would have laughed, too. Anyway, I happened to look around, and I saw a boy standing nearby watching the ducks, and me. And smiling. "Hi," he said.

I remember I just stood there, not saying anything. He was an awfully handsome boy; tall, black hair, with very brown, penetrating eyes. He was obviously Spanish—I guess that's why I didn't answer him right away. Don't stop me with that frown—I know that feeling is wrong, but I can't help the way I feel, can I?

Well, anyway, I just stood there, staring at the ducks, trying to ignore the boy, hoping he'd go away. I guess my displeasure was obvious, because he jammed his hands into his coat pockets and took a step backwards.

"Look," he said, "I didn't mean to be forward. Honest. It's just that I don't see a girl staring at ducks everyday—that's all. I'm sorry."

I felt bad. "You like to watch the ducks?" I asked.

"Yeah."

"You come everyday?"

"Most everyday," he said. He walked towards me. It's funny. The thing that sticks most in my mind about that first time was his coat. He had on this trench coat, all frayed around the collar and cuffs with only one button on it. Silly to be so impressed by a coat.

"I like it here," he said.

"Why?"

"The quiet, I guess. I like the openness of it, the color. And you know, you can walk all around this park everyday, and the next day you come back and never remember a thing you saw the day before. You know that?"

I just stood there and nodded. Close up, he looked awfully strong. His shoulders were broad—from the funny way I stood there and looked at him, those shoulders seemed to span the breadth between that tree and the one over there.

He looked at me seriously. "Those ducks remind you of anyone you know?"

I laughed. I couldn't help but like him from that point on. We started talking about school and stuff—his and mine—you know, the stuff everybody talks about. We went up and sat on those flat rocks that surround the pond. We sat on those gritty rocks and just talked. Funny about Rick —that's his name—he used to talk with his hands and eyes. He had wide, strong hands, and great expressive eyes like you've never seen before. You could just sit there listening to him talking about the multiplication tables, fascinated by those hands and eyes. I wish I could remember exactly what we talked about that first time, because I'd like for you to get to know him as well as I did. He was unique in the way he expressed himself, the things he said. I don't think I can really explain to you what I learned from him and about him that first time. He was very Spanish, I could tell. His sentences were interspersed with *"buenos"* instead of "o.k.'s" and his words turned up at the end.

I was very interested in him, and in my excitement I dropped that awful English novel into the pond. He fished it out for me and said, *"Aqui, chulanita."* You know how some phrases stick in your mind? Well, that one did. That was the first of lots of times he called me *chulanita.*

I liked it, but I never knew what it meant. I don't think I wanted to know. Finally, I got up to leave.

I came back to the pond the next day. I half expected to see him, half not. Well, he came. Only this time we walked. For hours it must have been. Then we came to this tree—the same one you and I are under now—and rested. Only then it was red and brown and orange. See those lines on its trunk? Does that look like a face to you? Well, it didn't to me either. But it did to Rick. He called that ridiculous face Dr. Woppsie and we talked to it every time we sat under this tree. . . .

Rick and I were together a lot after those first two meetings. We were at the park practically all the time. We never got around to actually dating one another, and I guess the reason why is the reason why I'm bothering at all to explain this whole thing.

Do you know what a person's being Spanish means? It began to mean nothing to me. I was fascinated by his mannerisms, his speech, his family traditions. But you know how adults and other people can say things in a way that you want to scream?

Let me tell you.

Rick had asked me to come home with him and meet his family. I was thrilled. He talked about his parents all the time and I wanted so very much to meet them.

"Come home with me first," I said, "to ask."

When we got to my house, we walked in the back door and my mother was in the kitchen putting hamburger together for supper. Mother had never met him before. I had talked about him a lot, but I never mentioned that he was Spanish. I don't know why really. Yes, I do know why. . . .

When I introduced Rick to her, she looked up at him, and said hello. Her tone was cool, and she kept on molding that awful red meat in her hands. I think that's the cruelest thing my mother has ever done—molding that raw meat in her hands while he just stood there. I put my hand on the edge of the sink and saw her rather obvious disapproval through waves of hatred for her.

Rick was uncomfortable. I didn't even ask her, we just left . . . Are you beginning to understand?

And then, one day in the park as I noticed the fading colors telling me of the coming winter, I saw two friends from school.

Sally and Beth were my good friends. We'd shared nearly twelve years of school. I was waiting for Rick, I can remember. To this day I don't know what they were doing there, under our tree, but there they were.

The three of us just stood there talking. Finally, Rick came up and I introduced him. I felt a change in the conversation. Beth began to look at her watch; Sally's hands seemed suddenly nervous. I began to get this funny feeling in my stomach. All their strained words seemed like echoes to me. Gradually I couldn't hear them at all. But I can remember muttering something to Rick about it being late and I'd better go on with Sally and Beth. He nodded, and I noticed a strange look in his eyes.

Sally and Beth and I turned and started the walk home. I didn't look back at Rick. Sally and Beth's words fell around me. But I caught Beth saying, "Lord—how could you do it? You desperate for company or something?"

There was that feeling in my stomach again. But listen. Do you know what I said to her? Do you know how I answered her? "I guess so," I said. "He's just some fellow I met. You know."

Beth and Sally laughed. Sally looked relieved. "Boy, you know what that could do to a girl's reputation. His being, well, Mexican and all."

She said that one word as if it were dirty, but I didn't notice that then. I just nodded. I said, "Wait a minute for me, won't you? I'll be right back."

I wouldn't wait for their questions. I turned and ran back towards the tree, quickly to catch Rick. As I ran, the fading autumn colors whizzed past me. I can't remember objects—only fading color. I saw him ahead. He had his hands jammed into his pockets when I finally caught up with him.

"Rick."

He turned.

"I'm sorry. I just wanted to say . . . well . . . good-by."

He just stood there framed by the fading color. We must have stood there two whole minutes, me trying to avoid those eyes and fading color.

"Chulanita," he said. "Good-by."

He turned and walked slowly away, broad shoulders and frayed collar blurred. The fading color blurred. Everything blurred in tears as I ran back to Beth and Sally. . . .

I'm finished now. I feel numb. Telling you this has made me feel a little better—but not much. I keep remembering Rick. I keep asking myself, "Did I make a mistake? Wasn't I cruel?" *What do you think?* Is there any other way in the world—as it is today? *

In an essay called "Of Experience," Emerson wrote: "All writing comes by the grace of God, and all doing and having." I cannot explain to you the tremendous lift I get from putting thoughts into lasting form, just as you cannot perfectly describe

* Reprinted from *Ingenue* Magazine, October, 1962.

your feelings to me. We call ourselves writers, but when we attempt to discuss our craft, words will not come. In our soul-searching, however, we know that satisfaction is there, as sure as the passing breeze and the grace of God.

Chapter X

ANY QUESTIONS?

Without knowing the force of words, it is impossible to know men.

—Confucius

When a teacher comes to the end of a class period, she usually asks, "Any questions?" Having thought that she had covered every angle of the subject, she is surprised that so many questions are unanswered in the minds of her students. No doubt this book has left unsaid many facets of writing. Some of them you will learn through your own writing, some through reading. No one has all of the answers for every individual because writing is not a mechanical process; it is a creative experience that differs for each person. Here are a few topics that free lancers have asked me to discuss:

1. *How long should I stay with second-class markets before I try the top ones?* As you increase your output, try top markets occasionally. If you always get printed rejection slips, you know your material is not quite ready. I would say that at least two years of fairly regular selling to smaller magazines is necessary before you can write well enough for bigger publications.

2. *What are "rights?"* As a general rule, when you endorse your check from a magazine you are selling all rights to your manuscript. The Methodist Publishing House attaches a form to the check that states:

> By endorsement of this check the payee (1) conveys to the Methodist Publishing House the rights to the material described and as

> stated above, and (2) certifies that he is in legal possession of the rights conveyed and has full authority to execute this conveyance.

In this case, if your article is reprinted in another magazine, you will not be paid for it a second time.

The American Baptist Publication Society sends a card of acceptance with the following notation on the bottom of it:

> The acceptance of our check will be understood as your acknowledgment of payment in full for ALL RIGHTS. You may reserve book rights, but you are not free to sell second rights on this material unless there has been a written agreement to that effect. You will receive a copy of the periodical in which it appears.

Some confession magazines require that you return a signed, notarized affidavit to the effect that your material is original and that you are giving up all rights to it. As a free-lance article writer you need not be concerned about rights, but if you go into writing books, plays, or short stories, it is best to consult a lawyer before signing any legal forms.

3. *Do you count every word on a page?* No. I count the average number of words in a line and multiply by the number of lines on a page, then multiply by the total number of pages. For example, my typewriter turns out approximately 200 words per page. If a manuscript is five pages long, the article is 1,000 words. (It is the mark of an amateur to put the exact number of words on his cover sheet, such as 1,372.)

4. *What is plagiarism?* To steal the ideas, words or writings of someone else and to pass them off as one's own is plagiarism. One magazine discontinued contests because so many of the manuscripts were plagiarized; so-called authors copied material from old publications and submitted it as their own. Never copy someone else's writings, because to do so is morally wrong and you will be sure to be found out. That takes the fun out of writing, anyway, for the most enjoyment a writer has is in presenting his own views in a way that no one else could.

5. *Should "I" be avoided in article writing?* No. At one time we heard the advice, "Keep yourself out of the article." During

World War II, however, readers were presented more than ever before with factual material in the on-the-spot, I-was-there manner of Ernie Pyle. The personal touch has carried over into article writing, and it gives an authenticity and immediacy to your subject matter that readers respond to more warmly than they do to formal writing. I put myself into 95 percent of my articles.

6. *Suppose I have a manuscript partially finished, but I do not want to put any more work on it until an editor is interested in the idea. May I query several editors at once?* No. Send only one letter of query at a time. You would be on the spot if two editors sent you airmail letters requesting the manuscript. That happened to one free-lance writer I know. Luckily, the first editor she sent her query to was prompt in answering her and he returned her manuscript before too much time had elapsed to submit it to the second one, but she spent several uncomfortable days waiting for the outcome.

7. *Writing is referred to as a "business," a "craft," a "profession," and a "trade." Which is it?* Writing is a "business" because it is a commercial enterprise when you sell your product and keep business-like records. It can be called a "craft" because it requires art or skill. It is a "profession" in the sense that it is a calling, an occupation to which you devote yourself. It is also a "trade," the business you practice or the work you engage in on a regular basis.

8. *Should I delay writing for money until I have studied more?* No. Start today. You learn to write by writing. A writer reads and writes every day. You study on your own as you go along. At the end of this chapter there is a list of books that will tell you how other writers work.

Persons vary in their ability to observe life, to select important details, to record them, and to interpret their meaning. Every writer, famous or unknown, has one undeniable characteristic, though: perseverance. He sticks "doggedly" to writing.

When you start at the bottom of the ladder, there is no place to go except on up to the top, a rung at a time. Happy climbing!

RECOMMENDED READING

Archer, Jules, *I Sell What I Write,* Frederick Fell, Inc., New York, 1950.

Armour, Richard, *Writing Light Verse,* The Writer, Inc., Boston, Mass., 1947, 1958.

Blackiston, Elliott, *Short Story Writing for Profit,* The Writer, Inc. Boston, 1937.

Bower, Warren (Editor), *How to Write for Pleasure and Profit,* J. B. Lippincott Co., Philadelphia and New York, 1950.

Brande, Dorothea, *Becoming a Writer,* Harcourt Brace & Co., New York, 1934.

Burack, A. S., *The Writer's Handbook,* The Writer, Inc., Boston, Mass., 1953.

Campbell, Walter S., *Writing: Advice and Devices,* Doubleday & Co., Inc., Garden City, New York, 1956.

Cole, Toby, *Playwrights on Playwriting,* Hill & Wang, New York, 1960.

Cox, Sidney, *Indirections for Those Who Want to Write,* Alfred A. Knopf, New York, 1947.

Elwood, Maren, *111 Dont's for Writers,* The Writer, Inc., Boston, Mass., 1949.

Elwood, Maren, *Write the Short Short,* The Writer, Inc., Boston, Mass., 1947.

Engle, Paul, *On Creative Writing,* E. P. Dutton & Co., Inc., New York, 1964.

Farrar, Larston, *How to Make $18,000 a Year Free-lance Writing,* Hawthorn Books, Inc., New York, 1957, 1960.

Farrar, Larston, *Successful Writers and How They Work,* Hawthorn Books, Inc., New York, 1959.

Flesch, Rudolf, *A New Way to Better English,* Harper & Bros., New York, 1958.

Fox, Edward S., *How to Write Stories That Sell,* The Writer, Inc., Boston, Mass., 1961.

Garrison, Roger H., *A Guide to Creative Writing,* Henry Holt & Co., New York, 1951.

Gosnell, Janice and Powell, Mary Allen, *Christian Writer's Handbook,* Christian Writers Institute, Chicago, Ill., 1961.

Gunning, Robert, *The Technique of Clear Writing,* McGraw-Hill Book Co., Inc., New York, 1952.

Henry, Omer, *Writing and Selling Magazine Articles,* The Writer, Inc., Boston, Mass., 1962.

Hilliard, Robert L., *Writing for Television and Radio,* Hastings House, New York, 1962.

Klare, George R. and Buck, Byron, *Know Your Reader,* Hermitage House, New York, 1954.

Lambuth, David, *The Golden Book on Writing,* The Viking Press, New York, 1963.

Manners, William, *Wake Up and Write,* Arc Editions, New York, 1962. (Paperback)

Mathieu, Aron, *The Creative Writer,* Writer's Digest, Cincinnati, Ohio, 1961.

McCleary, Dorothy, *Creative Fiction Writing,* The Writer, Inc., Boston, Mass., 1947.

Meredith, Scott, *Writing to Sell,* Harper & Bros., New York, 1950.

Morris, Terry, *Prose by Professionals,* Doubleday & Co., Garden City, New York, 1961.

Orvis, Mary Burchard, *The Art of Writing Fiction,* Prentice-Hall, Inc., New York, 1948.

Reynolds, Paul R., *The Writer and His Markets,* Doubleday & Co., Inc., Garden City, New York, 1959.

Strunk, William, Jr., *Elements of Style,* The Macmillan Co., New York, 1959.

Targ, William, *A Reader for Writers,* Hermitage House, New York, 1951.

Uzzell, Thomas H., *Technique of the Novel,* The Citadel Press, New York, revised edition 1959.

Weisbord, Marvin, *A Treasury of Tips for Writers,* Writer's Digest, Cincinnati, Ohio, 1965.

Wilson, Barbara Ker, *Writing for Children,* Franklin Watts, Inc., New York, 1960.